The REAL Man Program

Flyers, Handouts, & Worksheets

ARE YOU FOR *REAL* ?

If You Want To Be A
~ REAL Man ~

There are a lot of myths in our society about what it means to be a real man. Contrary to popular belief, being a man is not about how strong and muscular you are; it's not about what kind of car you drive; it's not about how much money you have, or about how many women you can use.

Life is not about money, cars, fame, physical appearance, and women. It's about who you are as a person; it's about the way you live your life; and it's about how you treat other people.

When it comes right down to it…

Being a **REAL** man means that you:

R-espect all people,

E-specially women.

A-lways do the right thing.

L-ive a life that matters.

1st and 10: The 10 Facts and Fictions of Manhood

Dispelling the Myths & Promoting the Truth of What It Means to Be a Real Man

Sorting Out the Fact from the Fiction

There are a lot of myths out there about what it means to be a real man. There are a lot of false ideas that culture gives us; there are a lot of lies that our society tells us about what really makes a man. So, how do we sort through what's true and what isn't? How do we figure out what's *real* and what isn't? The following are myths that our society tells us about being a man… Let's sort through the myths and the mixed-messages, let's cut through the clutter and cultural lies, and let's sort out the facts from the fiction.

Fiction #1: Having a lot of money makes you a real man.

Fact: The truth is… What defines you as a man is not your individual wealth, but your *personal worth*. What defines you as a person is who you are on the inside. Being a real man has nothing to do with about how much money you make or have. It is about who you are, and how you live your life. **Your dignity defines you as a man.**

Fiction #2: Being popular makes you a real man.

Fact: The truth is… What defines you as a man is not how much other people like you or worship you. What defines you as a man is how much you can look yourself in the mirror and like what you see. Your popularity does not define you as a man. **Your integrity defines you as a man.**

Fiction #3: Being popular with the ladies makes you a real man.

Fact: The truth is… What defines you as a man is not how many women like you. It is not about how many women want to be with you, or how many women want to sleep with you. Being a real man has nothing to do with how many women you can get with. It is about what kind of a man you are; it is about how well you treat people—all people: *especially* women. Your vitality does not define you as a man. **Your virtue defines you as a man.**

Fiction #4: Having a lot of "swag" (material possessions) makes you a real man.

Fact: The truth is… What defines you as a man is not how much style or "swag" you have. It is not about how much money you can flash, or about how much jewelry you can show off. What defines you as a man is the way you carry yourself. Being a real man has nothing to do with what kind of clothes you wear, or about how much cash you can flash. Being a real man is about having self-respect and carrying yourself with class. Your style does not define you. Your substance does. Your "swag" does not define you as a man. **Your *self-respect* and *class* define you as a man.**

Fiction #5: Being violent and aggressive towards others makes you a real man.

Fact: The truth is… What defines you as a man is not how rough and tough you can be with others. Being a real man has nothing to do with how violent or aggressive you are be toward others. Being a real man has nothing to do with hurting others. Being hurtful doesn't make you a tough guy. It makes you a thug. Being harmful doesn't get you respect. Being *helpful* does. Being violent and intimidating doesn't make you a man. Being patient and tempered does. Hurting people has nothing to do with being a real man. Your temper does not define you as a man; your *temperance* does. Your ability to keep your composure—to show that you have true power over yourself—makes you a real man. Your ability to remain calm and to stay cool—to demonstrate that you have true power to control yourself and to consider your actions—makes you a *real* man. Your anger does not define you as a man. **Your self-control defines you as a man.**

Fiction #6: Being violent and aggressive towards women makes you a real man.

Fact: The truth is… What defines you as a man is not how rough and tough you can be with women. Being a real man has nothing to do with hitting or intimidating a woman. It has to do with being kind and gentle and patient. It has to do with being tender and understanding. Being a real man has nothing to do with controlling or restraining a woman; it has *everything* to do with controlling and restraining yourself. Being hurtful doesn't make you a real man; being *helpful* does. Being harmful doesn't gain you any respect from women; being *heart-felt* does. Your rage does not define you as a man. **Your self-restraint defines you as a man.**

Fiction #7: Drinking alcohol or doing drugs makes you a real man.
Fact: The truth is… What defines you as a man is not how much you can drink, or how often you smoke. It's about *taking care of your body*, and it's about *making good decisions* – making *successful* decisions. Drinking alcohol doesn't make you look tough. It makes you look childish. Using drubs doesn't make you look cool. It makes you look foolish. Using alcohol, drugs, or tobacco is a bad idea. It's dumb. It's stupid. It will get you in trouble, and it will prevent you from becoming successful. Drugs and alcohol do not define you as a man. **Your decisions define you as a man.**
And the better your decisions, the better type of man you will be.

Fiction #8: Having a reputation makes you a real man.
Fact: The truth is… What defines you is not how many possessions you can amass, or how many people you can surpass; it is how much respect and admiration you can earn, and how much you can do to help others. What defines you as a man is not what other people think about you, but what you think about yourself. What defines you as a man is not what other people say about you, but what you know in your heart is true. It is not about who other people think or say you are, but about who you know deep down that you really are. Your reputation does not define you as a man. **Your character defines you as a man.**

Fiction #9: Being able to Bench-Press a lot makes you a real man.
Fact: The truth is… What defines you as a man is not how much weight you can bench-press off your chest, or about how big your chest is or how cut your pec's are. Being a real man has nothing to do with how much weight you can bench. It has nothing to do with how big and muscular you are, or about how strong and tough you look. It's not about how tough you are in muscle, but how tough you are in spirit— it's not the size of your chest, but the size of the heart that beats inside your chest. Being a real man is about having a tough mind and a tender heart. It is about having principles, and more importantly, *living by your principles*. It is about working hard and competing against *yourself*, and more importantly, *being helpful and compassionate toward others*. Your performance in the gym does not define you as a man. **Your principles define you as a man.**

Fiction #10: Being a great athlete makes you a real man.
Fact: The truth is… What defines you as a man is not how many plays you can make, or how many points you can score on a court. What defines you as a man is how you play the game, and more importantly, how you play the Game of Life. What defines you as a man is not how many touchdowns you score, how many passes you complete, or how many tackles you make on Friday night. What defines you as a man is not how many times you get your name in the newspaper, how many of your clips make it onto the internet, or how pats on the back you receive in the hallways at school. What defines you as a man is *the way that you play the game*, and more importantly, the *way that you live your life*. Your touchdowns do not define you as a man. **Your honor defines you as a man.**

~ These are the 10 fictions and falsehoods of manhood, and we must learn to address and to fix them all first, before we can learn to come together as a *Human Team*, and build a better world.

The Truth, the Whole Truth, & Nothing but the Truth
If you want the truth—the whole truth, and nothing but the truth—
If you want the <u>real deal</u> on what it means to be a <u>real man</u>… then here it is:
What defines you as a man is ***who you are*** and ***how you live your life***.

When it comes right down to it, being a "<u>Real</u>" man means that you…

R.espect all people,
  E.specially women,
    A.lways do the right thing.
      L.ive a life that matters.

The Questions is: "Are *you* for **REAL**?"
Stand Up & Stand Tall…
Be a REAL Man!
Make a REAL Difference!

THE 4 QUARTERS OF MANHOOD

Respect all people

Being a *real* man is about treating *all* people with respect and dignity. The golden rule is simple enough, and true enough that virtually every religion and ideology in the world deems it one of its most important values. Treat everyone the way you'd want to be treated…period.
You can tell virtually all you need to know about a man by the way he treats others.

Especially women

Being a *real* man is all about treating women with respect—plain and simple. Be a gentleman at all times, and always be respectful. You can tell just about everything you need to know about a man by the way he treats a woman.

Always do the right thing

Being a *real* man is about having principles and living by those principles. It is about having something called "consistent character," which means that you have the same principles, regardless of the circumstances. It is incredible how much good you can do, and how many difficult situations you can make it through in life if you just live by five simple words: *Always do the right thing.*

Live a life that matters.

Being a *real* man is about striving for excellence in every aspect of life. It is about always doing your very best to reach your full potential in this world: to make the most of your talents, opportunities, and potential to impact others in a positive way. Being a *real* man is about investing yourself in your own success, and more importantly, in the success of others.

Be a **REAL** Man!

Live by the Golden Rule

The Golden Rule

The golden rule is simple enough, and true enough, that virtually every religion and ideology in the world deems it as one of its most important values. Treat everyone the way you'd want to be treated…plain and simple. Live by the golden rule, and always show respect to others. You can tell virtually all you need to know about a man by the way he treats other people.

The Golden Rule is a foundational principle of many of the world's major religions and philosophies. Below are versions of the rule from some of the various belief systems and cultures in this great world of ours.

Judaism
"What is hateful to you, do not do to your neighbor:
that is the whole of the Torah; all the rest of it is commentary." ~ *The Talmud*

Christianity
"In everything, do unto others as you would have them do unto you;
for this sums up the Law and the Prophets." ~ *The Gospel of Matthew 7:12*

Islam
"Not one of you is a believer until he loves for his brother what
he loves for himself." ~ *The Fortieth Hadith of an-Nawawi 13*

Hinduism
"This is the sum of duty: do naught unto others
that which would cause you pain if done to you." ~ *The Mahabharata*

Buddhism
"Hurt not others in ways you yourself would find hurtful." ~ *Udana-Varga, 5:18*

Zoroastrianism
"That nature alone is good which refrains from doing unto another
whatsoever is not good for itself." ~ *Dadistan-I-Dinik, 94:5*

Jainism
"A man should wander about treating all creatures
as he himself would be treated." ~ *Sutrakritanga 1:11:33*

Western Tradition
"Treat others the way that you yourself would want to be treated."
~ *The words of parents, teachers, and mentors everywhere*

~

Do good to all. Do harm to none.
This is the formula for achieving harmony in life.

Some Other Important Rules

The Golden Rule states that you should treat others the way you would want others to treat you. But the Golden Rule, however, is not the only important rule that there is. Here are a few additional rules to consider for treating other people with respect:

The Silver Rule

If the Golden Rule states:
Treat others the way that you would want to be treated.
— Or —
Do unto others as you would have others do unto you.

Then the Silver Rule complements it by stating:
*Do **not** do unto others as you would **not** have others do unto you.*
— Or —
*Do **not** do to other people, what you would **not** want them to do to you.*
To take it one step further: Do not do—or say—to other people what you would not want them to do, or say, to you.
~
"What is hateful to you, do not do to your fellow man."

~ Hillel the Elder

The Bronze Rule

The Bronze Rule states:
*Treat others the way you would want the person you **loved most** to be treated.*
— Or —
*Treat others the way you would want your **favorite person** to be treated.*

We all have people whom we care about deeply, and whom we respect a great deal. Whether it is a mother, a father, a favorite teacher or a coach, a sister, a girlfriend, or a best friend… the fact is that we would never want anyone to do or say anything that might hurt that person in any way. If you would treat other people as if they were the one person you cared about most in this world… then you would be upholding the spirit of the Bronze Rule.

The Titanium Rule

Finally, there is the Titanium Rule.
The Titanium Rule gets its name for one reason: because,
like the strong alloy known that it is named after, the Titanium Rule is *bulletproof*. Meaning, that if you follow it, then you cannot help but to act respectfully toward others.

The Titanium Rule states:
*Treat other people the way you would want
your own **mother** to be treated.*

It's All About Respect.
Respect of all kinds. Respect at all times.
Respect on all days. Respect in all ways.
Respect, Respect, Respect ... Always.

~

It's All
About Respect.
Respect of all kinds.
Respect at all times.
Respect on all days.
Respect in all ways.
Respect: Always.

~

The Rules of Respect

The following rules will guide our behaviors and interactions with one another throughout the entire program. The "Rules of Respect" are to help us create the best environment we can to learn, grow, and strive toward reaching our full potential. The rules will help created this environment, and we will help to create the rules to begin with. Below are the official rules of our classroom and program. And remember: "The Rules of Respect" are always in effect.

The Rules of Respect

1.

2.

3.

4.

5.

6.

7.

8.

9.

10.

11.

12.

13.

14.

15.

It's All About RESPECT

The Rules of Respect … Are Always In Effect!

"Life Is Color-Blind: The Heroic Story of Joe Girardi"
(How one man's willingness to help save a life overcame the boundaries of difference)

New York Yankees manager, Joe Girardi was driving in his car on his way home, shortly after winning the 2009 World Series. While driving across New York City's famous George Washington Bridge, Girardi saw a car crash into the barrier on the other side of the road.

Knowing that someone could have been seriously injured, and that their life might be in serious danger as well, Girardi flung open his door and sprinted across five lanes of traffic, where he then proceeded to pull a middle-age, female driver from out of her badly-damaged car to safety. The nearby police officers came to the victim's aid as well. An ambulance unit was called to the scene, for what eventually turned out to be mere precautionary reasons.

Had it not been for Girardi's timely actions, the woman behind the wheel of that ill-fated automobile might have required more than just "precautionary" measures. She very well could have been seriously injured—or perhaps even worse. Maybe her car would have exploded, or perhaps another car or cars may accidentally have slammed into hers.

Joe Girardi was a real-life hero. But what is even more impressive than what he did, was the fact that he did it *without even knowing* the person he was saving. In fact, Girardi didn't know a single thing about the person he was risking his life to save. And yet, it didn't matter—not at all.

Joe Girardi did not stop to think about whether he should help the person in that car or not; he didn't stop to consider whom he was potentially going to help, before deciding to risk his life for another. He didn't even think about whether or not he would receive anything in return for his heroic efforts.

All that Joe Girardi cared about… was helping someone else who needed help. Girardi didn't know that person. He didn't know anything about that person. All Joe Girardi knew was that someone's life was in danger, and that he was in a position to help save it.

As it turns out, the victim of the car accident didn't know Joe Girardi either. She was a middle-aged woman, who wasn't even a baseball fan at all. For all she knew, the person saving her life was an average, everyday, non-famous person. But even if he was, it wouldn't have mattered. All that mattered to that woman, was that Girardi was there to help. And to Girardi, it wouldn't have mattered who that woman was… she could have been the biggest Boston Red Sox fan in the world… but at that moment in time, when her life was on the line, Girardi was willing to put aside any and every difference, in order to focus on something of far-greater importance: Life itself.

Joe Girardi didn't risk his life to help save another's, because it was the popular thing to do, or because he was going to become (even more) famous, or because he was going to get some kind of reward for it. No: Joe Girardi risked his life to help save another's for one, simple reason: because it was the right thing to do.

To Joe Girardi, it didn't matter who was driving that other car—all he knew was that a member of his human family was in trouble, and that he was the one person who could help. To the victim he saved, it didn't matter who Girardi was—whether he was a Yankee or not. All she knew was that he was there to save her life. (He was there to be her "guardian angel.") The rest was irrelevant.

If your life was on the line: would you really care who your Guardian Angel was?

Life Is Color-Blind … Shouldn't We Be Too?
Life does not care about race, creed, color, or ethnicity… neither does Death, for that matter. Life doesn't care about material wealth or social status; nor does it care about orientation or political views. Life does not care about any of these things, and neither should we. Life, itself, has no prejudices… and neither should we. To put it another way: *Life is color-blind… Shouldn't we be too?*

~ The sooner we realize that WE ARE ALL PEOPLE, the better off we will all be.

We should always strive to treat one another with respect. By being tolerant, civil, and respectful to all people at all times, we make the world a better and more pleasant place. By treating others the way that we, ourselves, would want to be treated, we will make this wonderful world of ours a much more peaceful and enjoyable place in which to live.

<u>Put Differences Aside:</u>
<u>It Makes No Difference To Me</u>
A poem about putting differences aside,
in order to focus on more important things in life

<u>It Makes No Difference To Me</u>

Your race, your color, your credit, your creed:
It makes no difference to me.
Respect in word, and honor in deed;
These, and Victory, are all that I seek.

I care not what color it is that you bleed:
It makes no difference to me.
So long as you spill it in toil—not for you nor me, but *we*.
These, and Victory, are all that I seek.

Your height, your weight, your leap, your speed,
It makes no difference to me.
Your will to strive, your effort to reach,
These, and Victory, are all that I seek.

I care not for what language you speak,
It makes no difference to me.
A bond not meek and a word not weak,
These, and Victory, are all that I seek.

Whose works, whose gain, whose fame may peak,
It makes no difference to me.
I long for honor and glory—not yours or mine—but *ours*, you see.
These, and Victory, are all that I seek.
...

Victory and Honor, are what matter you see.
The rest of it makes no difference to me.
Your word and your bond—not a grand applause;
Your best and your most, for a worthy cause;
Your head and your heart, and the truth that they speak…
These, and Victory, are all that I seek.

The Most Important Person You Will Ever Meet

The Most Important Person You Will Ever Meet

When your time in this world ends, and you are called up to your inevitable appointment at the entrance to the Pearly Gates (or wherever your afterworld may be), there is going to be someone standing there to greet you. That someone is going to be sitting there patiently waiting to ask you a single question. Your answer to that question is going to determine the rest of your eternity… because you see, that one person holds the key to the Gates, and he or she alone gets to choose whether to let you in or not.

The only catch is this: the person standing there is going to be the exact opposite of you in every way. They are going to be short if you are tall; they are going to have blond hair if you have dark or red hair; they are going to be fat if you are skinny, or be skinny if you are overweight.

That person is going to be black or Asian if you are white, or perhaps Middle-Eastern if you are Hispanic. They are going to be homosexual if you are straight. They're going to have a lot of tattoos or body piercings if you don't have any; they are going to be foreign or an immigrant if you are an American. They are going to be Muslim, or Atheist, or Hindu, or Jewish if you are a Christian; they are going to be devoutly religious if you are not. They are going to be a Boston Red Sox fan if you are a New York Yankees fan; they are going to be a Democrat if you are a Republican, or vice-versa. They are going to be poor if you are rich, or vice-versa. They are going to be a woman if you are a man, or vice-versa.

And when you arrive at the entrance way to Heaven (or to whatever afterlife you may believe in), the person that you meet there is going to look you squarely in the eye and ask you one thing… and one thing only…

How did you treat me?

~ Let's try to keep that in mind as we pass through this world with one another.

~

"Do not judge, or you too will be judged.
For in the same way you judge others, you will be judged…"
~ The Gospel of Matthew 7:1-2 (from the Christian Faith Tradition)

———————————————

Treat everyone as if they were the most important person
you were ever going to meet … because ultimately, they very well may be.

———————————————

"If you judge people, you have no time to love them."
~ Mother Theresa

People With A Healthy Self-Esteem

People with a healthy self-esteem are much more likely to develop the following positive aspects in themselves, to exhibit the following traits within themselves, and to experience the following positive aspects in their lives…

~ People with a healthy self-esteem are more likely to develop healthy and meaningful relationships. They are more likely to surround themselves with good people.

~ People with a healthy self-esteem are more likely to feel good about themselves. They are more likely to have the self-confidence necessary to take worthwhile and calculated risks; and they are more likely to have the courage and conviction to be proactive and to take the initiative when the time calls for it.

~ People with a healthy self-esteem are more resilient than most: they are more likely overcome obstacles and to make it through hard times; they are more likely to grow from periods of difficulty; and they are more likely to learn from their mistakes and setbacks, because they are more likely to view those experiences as learning tools and guideposts for future success. People with a healthy self-esteem are more resilient when it comes to dealing with adversity, and are thus more able and likely to overcome it.

~ People with a healthy self-esteem are more positive and optimistic. They are also more focused and determined in the efforts they undertake. People with a healthy self-esteem create high expectations for themselves. They set lofty goals, they work hard toward accomplishing those goals, and they continue to work and persevere until they achieve the goals they have set for themselves.

~ People with a healthy self-esteem have a strong sense of purpose. They are driven and determined, they attack each day and each opportunity with passion and purpose. They have an unquenchable desire to get the most out of themselves and out of their lives. People with a healthy self-esteem are confident, yet humble. They have a strong sense of positive pride, yet they always do their best to remain modest and level-headed.

~ People with a healthy self-esteem are more likely to be responsible for themselves and to others, they are more likely to be accountable for their actions and for the effects of those actions on others, and they are more likely to be respected and trusted by others as a result.

~ People with a healthy self-esteem are more likely to possess the qualities of mental toughness and self-discipline. They are more likely to lead themselves effectively, and they are more likely to lead other people successfully.

~ People with a healthy self-esteem are more likely to have a high level of integrity. They are more likely to exhibit a greater level of commitment in all that they do, and they are more likely to succeed in anything and everything they do.

~

"People who feel good about themselves stand tall,
hold their heads high, and are prone to succeed." ~ *Jean Conley*

People With A Healthy Self-Esteem

People with a healthy self-esteem are much more likely to develop the following positive aspects in themselves, to exhibit the following traits within themselves, and to experience the following positive aspects in their lives…

~ People with a healthy self-esteem are more likely to develop healthy and meaningful relationships. They are more likely to surround themselves with good people.

~ People with a healthy self-esteem are more likely to feel good about themselves. They are more likely to have the self-confidence necessary to take worthwhile and calculated risks; and they are more likely to have the courage and conviction to be proactive and to take the initiative when the time calls for it.

~ People with a healthy self-esteem are more resilient than most: they are more likely overcome obstacles and to make it through hard times; they are more likely to grow from periods of difficulty; and they are more likely to learn from their mistakes and setbacks, because they are more likely to view those experiences as learning tools and guideposts for future success. People with a healthy self-esteem are more resilient when it comes to dealing with adversity, and are thus more able and likely to overcome it.

~ People with a healthy self-esteem are more positive and optimistic. They are also more focused and determined in the efforts they undertake. People with a healthy self-esteem create high expectations for themselves. They set lofty goals, they work hard toward accomplishing those goals, and they continue to work and persevere until they achieve the goals they have set for themselves.

~ People with a healthy self-esteem have a strong sense of purpose. They are driven and determined, they attack each day and each opportunity with passion and purpose. They have an unquenchable desire to get the most out of themselves and out of their lives. People with a healthy self-esteem are confident, yet humble. They have a strong sense of positive pride, yet they always do their best to remain modest and level-headed.

~ People with a healthy self-esteem are more likely to be responsible for themselves and to others, they are more likely to be accountable for their actions and for the effects of those actions on others, and they are more likely to be respected and trusted by others as a result.

~ People with a healthy self-esteem are more likely to possess the qualities of mental toughness and self-discipline. They are more likely to lead themselves effectively, and they are more likely to lead other people successfully.

~ People with a healthy self-esteem are more likely to have a high level of integrity. They are more likely to exhibit a greater level of commitment in all that they do, and they are more likely to succeed in anything and everything they do.

~

"People who feel good about themselves stand tall,
hold their heads high, and are prone to succeed." ~ Jean Conley

Personal Exercise: Developing A Healthy and Positive Self-Esteem

Having a healthy and positive self-esteem means having healthy and positive thoughts about yourself and about your life. It means thinking of all the good things about yourself; thinking of all the good things that you've done in the past (the things you have accomplished), and thinking of all the good things you can—and will—do in the future. It means believing in yourself, and believing in the possibilities that the future holds for you.

Step One: Think of All the Good Things About You
What are your best qualities? What are your favorite things about yourself?
Make a list of the 5 things you like most about yourself:

1.
2.
3.
4.
5.

Now, make a list of 5 MORE good things about yourself.

1.
2.
3.
4.
5.

Step Two: Think of All the Good Things That You Have Accomplished
What are your proudest accomplishments?
Make a list of 5 things that you have accomplished so far in your life:

1.
2.
3.
4.
5.

Step Three: Think of All the Good Things You Want To Accomplish In the Future
What are some of the things you want to accomplish in the future?
Make a list of 5 things that you would like to accomplish, or goals that you want to achieve.
Then, after each one, write whether or not you think you can accomplish them. Write the words: "Yes, I Can!" next to each goal you believe you can achieve, and that you believe is possible. (Keep in mind: "Anything Is Possible!")

1.
2.
3.
4.
5.

Having a healthy and positive self-esteem means believing in yourself, believing in your abilities, and believing in your future. It means believing that you can accomplish great things in the future, and believing that *you will* accomplish those things, too). *Having a positive self-esteem is the key to having a positive attitude. And having a positive attitude is the key to having a positive—and successful—life.*

"Build Each Other Up" Partner Exercise
A partner activity to help build self-esteem and self-confidence,
by pointing out the good things in one another.

Build Each Other Up

The purpose of this exercise is to help students build up their levels of self-esteem and self-confidence by building up their classmate in the process. The objective is to promote feelings of self-value and self-worth, by promoting and pointing out the good qualities of each individual. It always feels good to hear compliments from others; and what is even better, is to be made aware of positive things that you didn't even know were there to begin with. The goal of this exercise is not only to raise awareness of the positive traits and characteristics that each person possesses, but also to help raise the levels of self-esteem, self-confidence, self-acceptance, and self-love of all the participants involved.

Steps Forward

Think of 10 good things about your partner: 10 really great things about them, about who they are, about how they look, about any positive characteristics they have, about any great things they have going for them. (What are their best qualities? What are your favorite things about them?)

Find 10 great things about the person… make sure they're really good!
Then, write down all 10 things that you come up with (below).

When you're done making your list… Share them with your partner.
Read each of the 10 positive things to your partner, and take your time: give each a chance to set in, and give your partner a chance to hear—and feel good—about each of those good things.

    1.
    2.
    3.
    4.
    5.
    6.
    7.
    8.
    9.
    10.

* **Bonus Round**: List 5 MORE great things about your partner. When you're done making your bonus list, read each of them to your partner, just like you did the first time.

    1.
    2.
    3.
    4.
    5.

Finishing Exercise: Go around the room and have each student read off 2 great things about their partner. (If time permits, you can have each student read the whole list.) It always feels good to be made to feel good by others; and it always feels even better to be made to feel good *in front of* others.

<u>A Great Analogy for Friendship</u>
What Building A House of Cards Can
Teach Us About Building Good Friendships

Good Friends Build Each Other Up… and Help Keep Each Other Up
What do people and playing-cards have in common? Well, more than you would think.
Remember back to when you were younger, and about how you used to try to build a house-of-cards, out of a deck of playing cards. More specifically, think about the first building blocks of the whole process: the very first two cards.

If you look at a playing card, it's very slight, thin, and frail. It's not strong enough to stand on its own. Now, you can try to make it stand up all by itself, but it will fall down immediately. It's just too flimsy to stay upright on its own.

You can try standing two cards up individually, side by side. However, once again, neither card is strong enough or sturdy enough to stand on its own, and therefore, each will always fall down if it only has its own weight to try to support itself.

Now, if you take those two cards and lean them against each other, something interesting happens: they suddenly become capable of standing, together, for a very long time. The reason this happens is because each card, flimsy and frail as it may be, is supporting the weight of the other. Neither is focusing all its energy on itself; instead, each is putting its energy toward supporting the other card.

In a lot of ways, we are just like those playing cards: none of us is strong enough to stand on our own; we each need help from one another. As much as we would like to believe that we are independent and that we're strong enough or sturdy enough to stand on our own, the truth is that we really do need the support of others to help keep us standing. And, just as we need others to be there for us, others **need us to be there for them**. That is the nature of our human world—that is how this life of ours works.

None of us is in this world alone. We're all in this together. We're all connected to one another in some way. We're all in this together, and therefore, we all have a responsibility to try to improve the lives of others as much as we possibly can. If we focus solely on ourselves and try to keep just ourselves up, then we will all fall down individually. However, **if we are there for one another, then it will all work out**.
~
It's amazing to look at an entire house of cards and realize that the whole structure is based on thin, flimsy little cards, none of which is strong enough to stand on its own. But, when you understand that each card is working to hold another up, and that another is there to provide help and support in return, then it all makes sense. When we all work to strengthen one another, we end up with an entire house being possible. Alone, none of us can stand. Together, we can all stand, and we can all stand as part of something that is far greater than ourselves.

~

"Lean on me, when you're not strong. I'll be your friend, I'll help you carry on.
For, it won't be long, till I'm gonna need somebody to lean on..."

~ *Lean On Me*, by Bill Withers

Go Out of Your Way to Do the Big Things for Other People: The Story of the Good Samaritan

The following is the story of the Good Samaritan; it is a famous and familiar story, about a man who stops to help someone in need. The passage is taken from the Gospel of Luke, found in chapter 10, verses 25-37. Although it originally comes from the New Testament portion of the Christian Bible, the story is one of universal application, and it can offer a valuable lesson to people of any religion or any culture.

On one occasion an expert in the law stood up to test Jesus. "Teacher," he asked, "what must I do to inherit eternal life?"

"What is written in the Law?" he replied. "How do you read it?"

*He answered: "Love the Lord your God with all your heart and with all your soul and with all your strength and with all your mind;" and, "**Love your neighbor as yourself.**"*

"You have answered correctly," Jesus replied. "Do this and you will live."

But he wanted to justify himself, so he asked Jesus, "And who is my neighbor?"

In reply Jesus said: "A man was going down from Jerusalem to Jericho, when he fell into the hands of robbers. They stripped him of his clothes, beat him and went away, leaving him half dead. A priest happened to be going down the same road, and when he saw the man, he passed by on the other side. So too, a Levite, when he came to the place and saw him, passed by on the other side. But a Samaritan, as he traveled, came where the man was; and when he saw him, he took pity on him. He went to him and bandaged his wounds, pouring on oil and wine. Then he put the man on his own donkey, took him to an inn and took care of him. The next day he took out two silver coins and gave them to the innkeeper. 'Look after him,' he said, 'and when I return, I will reimburse you for any extra expense you may have.'

*"Which of these three do you think was a neighbor to the man who fell into the hands of robbers?" The expert in the law replied, "The one who had mercy on him." Jesus told him, "**Go and do likewise.**"*

The lesson seems pretty simple: we should be compassionate to everyone and help those in need. But, if we look closer at the story, we'll find that it goes a little deeper than that. Case in point: let's look at things from the Samaritan's perspective, and let's think about how much he was risking in order to help someone he didn't even know…

Stopping in an unfamiliar area to help a stranger is a dangerous enough thing to do to begin with. Throw in the fact that the road from Jerusalem to Jericho is a steep, winding, remote, and narrow road that descends 3,600 feet through mountains and over a 17-mile route. For centuries, the road has been known as a place of robbers, and it is still considered dangerous even today. The *"Valley of the Shadow of Death"* is an actual location on the Jericho Road…that doesn't exactly sound like a safe place now does it? Added to all that, is the fact that the Samaritans and Jews essentially were sworn enemies.

So, not only did the Samaritan go out of his way to help someone in need, he risked his own safety, and maybe even his life, by stopping in a valley of thieves and criminals—where he very easily could have been robbed, beaten, and left for dead himself, just like the man he stopped to help. In addition, the Samaritan risked all of that for someone he didn't even know, and for someone who was a bitter enemy of his people.

It didn't matter that the man was Jewish; it didn't matter that doing the right thing might get the Samaritan hurt or robbed, or that it might cost him valuable time and money. What mattered was that a fellow human being needed his help.

Other people had passed by the victim, but were afraid to stop and help the man. Those people thought about the risk to themselves and they continued on their way, thinking "What will happen to *me* if I stop to help this man?" But the Samaritan saw the man and thought…
"What will happen to *THIS MAN* if I *don't* help him?"

~

"Every man is guilty of all the good he didn't do."

~ *Voltaire*

18

Be On the Lookout For Opportunities for Kindness

Be on the lookout for opportunities to perform acts of kindness. Always be thinking of ways you can help brighten someone's day; always be thinking of people who you can go out of your way to help.

Think of your friends, your loved ones, a neighbor, and a stranger… think about what you can do to help bring a little more joy to someone else's day. It doesn't have to be a big thing: it can be a small thing, a little thing, a tiny thing… *anything*. It doesn't have to be a big thing… it just has to be *some*thing.

Always be on the lookout for kindness. Always be thinking of some way to make someone else's day; always be thinking of someone you can help, someone you can help smile, and someone who you can make feel a little bit better about themselves, their life, or their day.

Kindness Challenge: Think about your friends, your neighbors, your classmates or your co-workers—is there someone who could use your help today? Is there someone who might be of a little help—or hope—from you today?

Be On the Lookout For Opportunities for Compliments

Be on the lookout for opportunities to pay someone a genuine compliment. Always be thinking of something you can say to help brighten someone's day. A little kind word or a phrase—maybe tell someone they have a nice outfit or a cute bag. Maybe tell them they have pretty eyes or a pretty smile. Maybe a tip of the cap and a wink… or even a simple "Thank You" will do. Always be looking for good things in people, and always be looking for ways to compliments those good things about other people. Always be asking yourself: "What can I compliment this person on?"

Compliment Challenge: Try to pay one, sincere compliment to each person you speak with today. (If you enjoy doing it—and if you enjoy seeing the smiles you create on other people's faces—then try it again tomorrow. But first, start with today. Pay one, honest and sincere compliment to each person you meet and interact with today.)

Be On the Lookout For Opportunities for Smiles

Be on the lookout for people in need of a smile. Always be looking for someone who might be in need of a smile. Always be looking for ways to help give someone that reason to smile. There are many people in our world—and in our daily lives—who don't have much at all to smile about. Some people need a smile of their own, and some people might even need to borrow a smile from you. Always do your best to try to give someone a reason to smile. Often the best way to do this, is to start by smiling yourself. Spread a little sunshine, and flash a big-bright smile. Give people a smile of their own, give them something to smile about… and start, by giving them a smile of your own.

Smile Challenge: Just for today… give a smile to each and every person you pass by or meet. Smile a big, bright, positive smile… full of cheerfulness and light. Greet everyone you meet with a smile. Give everyone you encounter your own smile. And don't just give them your smile… give them your *best* smile. (And again, if you enjoy doing it today—if you enjoy seeing the smiles you create on other people's faces—then try doing it again tomorrow. But first, start with today.) Give everyone you encounter your own smile. And don't just give them your smile… give them your *best* smile.

~ Be on the lookout: get up, get out, and reach out! Be on the lookout for opportunities for kindness.
~ Reach out to do something nice for someone, for no other reason but to help brighten their day.

A Little Bit of Kindness Goes a Long Way
No one's life is so perfect—or so free of stress—that they couldn't use a few extra words of kindness to help them along their way. No one's personal 'gas tank' is so full of energy and enthusiasm that they couldn't use a few encouraging words to help get them through the day.
~

No one has a perfect life. After all, everyone is working their way through a difficult and challenging world. We could all use a little help along the way.
~

Always be on the lookout to help brighten someone's day.
Always be ready and willing to go beyond the call of duty:
to go your of your way for the sake of another…
Go ahead: Make Someone's Day!

"The world needs a new kind of army:
an army of the Kind."
~ Anonymous

<u>Kindness Questions & Suggestions</u>
(Go Out of Your Way … To Make Someone's Day!)

<u>Kindness Questions</u>
1. What is the kindest thing anyone has ever done for you?
2. How did it make you feel? What made the action so kind?
3. List some other kind things that other people have done for you in the past month.
4. What is the kindest thing *you* have ever done for someone else?
5. How did it make you feel to do something like that for someone else?
6. Do you think it's possible that your kind act made you feel as good as the person you helped?

<u>Kindness Suggestions: Ideas for Kindness</u>
What are some things you can do to show kindness to other people?
Make a list of 10 nice things you can do for others this week… (They can be big things or small ones.)

1.	6.
2.	7.
3.	8.
4.	9.
5.	10.

<u>A Little More Kindness</u>
What are some little things you can do to make someone else's day? (For example: pay a compliment, write a nice letter or note, send a quick text message just to say hello, etc.)

1.	6.
2.	7.
3.	8.
4.	9.
5.	10.

<u>Big-Time Kindness: Go Out of Your Way… To Make Someone's Day!</u>
What are some "big things" you can do to *really* show kindness to others?
What are some things that you can do or say… to help make someone else's day?
(Here are some things to help get you thinking: Think about some of the kindest things you have ever done; think about some of the kindest things that other people have done for you.)

1.
2.
3.
4.
5.

Go Ahead …
Make Someone's Day!

Be Polite and Be Considerate

The following is a "Simple Acts of Kindness Tip-Sheet." It provides quick and easy ideas
for how to help show kindness to others, and to help make this world a kinder and better place.

~

Be polite and be considerate of others. Show respect to other people, be kind and courteous to those you
meet, and always do your best to do a little more than is necessary to help brighten someone's day… and
to help make someone's life a little better in some way.

What you can do to help make other people's lives better:

~ Smile and say hello to people you pass by.

~ Strike up a conversation with someone who seems down or lonely.

~ Eat lunch with a new student, a classmate, or someone who you don't normally see often or talk to.

~ Sit down next to someone who is sitting by themselves.

~ Spend time with someone who looks like they could use company.

~ Take a few moments to pass along a kind word or thoughtful note to a friend.

~ Send a thoughtful e-mail, write an encouraging note, or send a quick text message to someone.

~ Be there for a friend in need.

~ Listen to a friend in need, and let them know you care and are there for them.

~ Be there for anyone in need.

~ Listen to anyone in need, and let them know that you have hope for them.

~ Stick up for someone who is being picked on.

~ Stand up for someone who may not be able to stand up for themselves.

~ Do little things, so that other people won't have to be inconvenienced by having to do them
(flush toilets, wipe toilet seats, pick up trash that missed the trash can, put away dishes, clean dishes, etc.)

~ Do little things that take a minute, but that will be appreciated by others.

~ Let other people go before you: put others ahead of yourself… figuratively and *literally*.

~ Pass up the closest parking spot in the parking lot, so that another person can have it instead.

~ Help lighten other people's burdens in life…figuratively and *literally*.

~Help people out, and help people carry things too.).

~ Pick up something that another person drops.

~ Let someone know that dropped something, if they didn't notice it at first.

~ Return things that you borrow from other people.

~ Return things you find that belongs to other people.

~ Return money that you borrow from other people.

~ Return money you find that belongs to other people.

~ Say simple words like "please" and "thank you."

~ Say "you're welcome" and "my pleasure" as well.

~ Say respectful words like "sir" and "ma'am" when speaking with elders or authority figures.

~ Say words like "young lady" and "miss" … and say them with a smile.

~ Show your love and appreciation for your friends regularly.

~ Tell your friends that they are important to you, either via a quick text, or a phone call.

~ Build a bridge: Meet and make a new friend.

~ Rebuild an old bridge: Give an old friend a call who you haven't talked to in a while.

~ Repair and restore a bridge. Resolve a wounded friendship or repair an injured relationship.

~ Give people your quality time and your best attention.

~ Go out of your way to strike up a conversation with others.

~ Listen to what others have to say.

~ *Really* listen closely, and carefully, to what others have to say.

~ Remember what others have to say.

~ Give people the benefit of the doubt.

~ Look for the good in everyone you meet.

~ Help bring out the best in everyone you meet.

"Wherever there is a human being, there is an opportunity for kindness." ~ Seneca

"The power of kindness is immense. It is nothing less, really, than the power to change the world."
~ Daphne Rose Kingma

Do Something To Positively Affect Someone's Life Today

Go out of your way to help make someone else's day. Do something positive and do something good, for everyone you meet in life, and in all your travels along the way. Do something to make a positive difference each day. Do something to positively affect someone's life today.

~ Do something to positively affect someone's life today...

~ Do something good to have a positive impact on someone else's day.

~ Do something good for someone that you meet.

~ Do something good for *everyone* you meet.

~ Do something good for *anyone* you meet.

~ Do something good for other people, regardless of who they are.

~ Do something good for someone who you'll never see again.

~ Do something good for someone who will never have the opportunity to pay you back.

~ Do something good for *anyone*, without seeking *anything* for yourself in return.

~ Do something good for someone who will never know about it.

~ Do something to positively affect someone's life each day.

~ Do something to make someone else's day.

"Do something to positively affect someone's life today."
~ *Nick Saban (Head Football Coach: University of Alabama)*

The Impact of One Kind Deed
How One Act of Kindness Can Change a Person's Life

The Impact of One Kind Deed: *A Story from an Unknown Source*
One day, when I was a freshman in high school, I saw a kid from my class who was walking home from school. His name was Kyle. It looked like he was carrying all of his books. I thought to myself, "Why would anyone bring home all his books on a Friday? He must really be a nerd."

I had quite a weekend planned (parties and a football game with my friends tomorrow afternoon), so I shrugged my shoulders and went on. As I was walking, I saw a bunch of kids running toward him. They ran at him, knocking all his books out of his arms and tripping him so he landed in the dirt. His glasses went flying, and I saw them land in the grass about ten feet from him. He looked up and I saw this terrible sadness in his eyes. My heart went out to him. So, I jogged over to him and as he crawled around looking for his glasses, and I saw a tear in his eye. As I handed him his glasses, I said, "Those guys are jerks. They really should get lives." He looked at me and said, "Hey thanks!" There was a big smile on his face. It was one of those smiles that showed real gratitude.

I helped him pick up his books, and asked him where he lived. As it turned out, he lived near me, so I asked him why I had never seen him before. He said he had gone to private school before now. I would have never hung out with a private school kid before. We talked all the way home, and I carried some of his books. He turned out to be a pretty cool kid.

I asked him if he wanted to play a little football with my friends He said yes. We hung out all weekend and the more I got to know Kyle, the more I liked him, and my friends thought the same of him. Monday morning came, and there was Kyle with the huge stack of books again. I stopped him and said, "Boy, you are going to really build some serious muscles with this pile of books every day!" He just laughed and handed me half the books.

Over the next four years, Kyle and I became best friends. When we were seniors, we began to think about college. Kyle decided on Georgetown, and I was going to Duke. I knew that we would always be friends, that the miles would never be a problem. He was going to be a doctor, and I was going for business on a football scholarship.

Kyle was valedictorian of our class. I teased him all the time about being a nerd. He had to prepare a speech for graduation. I was so glad it wasn't me having to get up there and speak.

Graduation day, I saw Kyle. He looked great. He was one of those guys that really found himself during high school. He filled out and actually looked good in glasses. He had more dates than I had and all the girls loved him. Boy, sometimes I was jealous.

Today was one of those days. I could see that he was nervous about his speech. So, I smacked him on the back and said, "Hey, big guy, you'll be great!" He looked at me with one of those looks (the really grateful one) and smiled. "Thanks," he said. As he started his speech, he cleared his throat, and began "Graduation is a time to thank those who helped you make it through those tough years. Your parents, your teachers, your siblings, maybe a coach...but mostly your friends... I am here to tell all of you that being a friend to someone is the best gift you can give them.

"I am going to tell you a story. I just looked at my friend with disbelief as he told the story of the first day we met. He had planned to kill himself over the weekend. He talked of how he had cleaned out his locker so his Mom wouldn't have to do it later and was carrying his stuff home.
He looked hard at me and gave me a little smile.

"Thankfully, I was saved. My friend saved me from doing the unspeakable." I heard the gasp go through the crowd as this handsome, popular boy told us all about his weakest moment. I saw his mom and dad looking at me and smiling that same grateful smile. Not until that moment did I realize it's depth. Not until that moment did I realize the incredible impact of one simple, yet kind deed."

~
Never underestimate the impact of a kind deed,
and never overlook the power of compassion.
~

A Little Bit of Kindness Can Go A Very Long Way

The help of friends, and even the kindness of relative strangers, can go a very long way in helping to make a person's day, week, year, or even their life. Give of yourself whatever you can, whenever you can, and wherever you can. Do whatever it is that you can do, no matter how big or small a deed it may be. After all, you can never truly know how valuable your impact on another can be…
With one small gesture, you may/can change a person's life.

"Too often we underestimate the power of a touch, a smile, a kind word,
    a listening ear, an honest compliment, or the smallest act of caring,
      all of which have the potential to turn a life around."
      ~ Leo Buscaglia

Kindness Is Never In Vain

The good words we speak and the good deeds we do are never in vain.
They will always make their way into the hearts and minds of others.

The kind words we speak, and the good deeds we perform, are never in vain.
The good we do in this world always matters.
It never goes unnoticed, it never goes overlooked, and it never goes underappreciated.
What we do in this world matters.
What we do in our lives, counts for something in the lives of others.

No kind deed is ever in vain.
Every single act of kindness counts. Every small act of kindness matters.
Every little thing you do and say, indeed, makes a BIG difference.

Someone Needs Your Kindness Today

Somewhere, there is someone who needs your help.
Somewhere, there is someone who needs your helping hand.
Somewhere, there is someone who needs your encouraging words.
Somewhere, there is someone who needs your kindness and love.
Somewhere, there is someone who needs your healing and hope

Someone, somewhere, needs your presence.
Someone, somewhere, needs your assistance.
Someone, somewhere, needs your guidance.
Someone, somewhere, needs your deliverance.

Someone, somewhere, needs your help.
Someone, somewhere, needs your hope.
Someone, somewhere, needs your touch.
Someone, somewhere, needs your love.

"Throw out the lifeline across the dark wave—someone is sinking today."
~ Henry Milman

Experiencing & Expressing Gratitude

Gratitude is about understanding the good things and the good people you have in your life. Showing gratitude is about recognizing those things and those people, and expressing your appreciation for them and to them. Below are some questions to help you develop more of an "Attitude of Gratitude."

What are five things that you are grateful for in your life?
"I am grateful for…"

1.
2.
3.
4.
5.

What are five *more* things that you are grateful for in your life?
"I am grateful for…"

1.
2.
3.
4.
5.

Who are five PEOPLE you are grateful for in your life?
"I am grateful for…"

1.
2.
3.
4.
5.

What about each person are you grateful for?
Write one specific thing you are grateful for, next to each person's name (above).

What can you do to show your gratitude to others?
What are some things you can do to let people know that you are grateful to them?
(Here are some hints: Tell them—say "thank you." Give them a hug or a handshake. Pay someone a genuine compliment. Send a 'Thank You' note (or an e-mail, or a text message). Give them a phone call, write a quick e-mail, post on their Facebook or MySpace page, etc.). Try to come up with at least five things… or more if you can. (The more ways you can express your gratitude, the better!)
"I can show my gratitude to people by…"

1.	6.
2.	7.
3.	8.
4.	9.
5.	10.

Who Makes *Your* Day?
Who are some people who have shown kindness to you recently?
Who has gone out of their way, to help make *your* day?

Who Makes Your Day... Possible?
Who makes it possible for you to get through and enjoy each day? (Who makes your day... and who makes your bed that you sleep on; who makes your breakfast that you eat in the morning; who makes your car or the bus that you get on; who makes your lunch; who makes everything else that is part of your day; who makes you day possible; who makes your day good; who makes your day better; and who makes your day great?

Think about all the people who help to make your day... possible... good... better... and great.
List as many people as you can:

1.	6.	11.
2.	7.	12.
3.	8.	13.
4.	9.	14.
5.	10.	15.

Who Makes Your Day... Good?
Choose one person who really makes your day good?

Who Makes Your Day... Even Better?
Choose one person who really makes your better?

Who Makes Your Day... Great?
Choose one person who really makes your day great?

More Gratitude Questions
1. Do you show appreciation for the important people in your life?
2. Do you feel like you do it often enough?
3. What are some ways that you show appreciation for the special people in your life?
   (People like: Your parents, your family, your teachers and coaches, your friends, etc.)
4. What are some things you can do to show appreciation to these people?
   What can you say? What can you do?

Who makes your day?   Who makes your day... possible?   Who makes your day... good?
Who makes your day... even better?   Who makes your day... *great*?
If you know it... make sure you show it!

Who makes *your* day... and do you make sure they *know* it?
Do you make sure to tell them?

Ways to Show Gratitude to Your Parents

Here are some ideas and suggestions to help you start thinking about gratitude,
and to help "get a move on" being grateful to your parents for all that they do for you:

Make A Move: Start Thinking about Things to Be Grateful to Your Parents For

Here are a few things to think about, when thinking about what to be grateful to your parents for:

1. What are some of the challenges and obstacles your parents faced when raising you?
2. What are some sacrifices your parents have had to make in order to help raise you?
3. What are some sacrifices your parents make every day to help take care of you?
4. What are some sacrifices your parents make every day to help you become successful?

Make A List

Make a list of at least 10 things you are grateful to your parents for:

1.   6.
2.   7.
3.   8.
4.   9.
5.   10.

Make An Effort

How often do you tell your parents that you are grateful for the things they do? Do you ever?
What are some things you are grateful for, that you haven't told your parents about yet?
Pick 5 things that you haven't showed your appreciation for yet. Then, make an effort
to tell these five things to your parents the next time you see them:

1.
2.
3.
4.
5.

Make Gratitude An Attitude

When it comes to being thankful to your parents, here is a great suggestion: make *gratitude* an *attitude*.
In other words… Have an Attitude of Gratitude.

Develop an Attitude of Gratitude: Think your parents for everything they do for you… for everything
they have done for you in the past… and for everything that they continue to do for you in the present.

Display an Attitude of Gratitude: *Thank* your parents for everything they do for you… for everything
they have done for you in the past… and for everything that they continue to do for you in the present.

Don't Stop Displaying that Attitude of Gratitude – Keep It Up: Show your appreciation for your
parents by telling them how grateful you are for the sacrifices that they make, and for everything they
have done to help you succeed. (Don't worry about how it sounds, or if you don't think it's "*manly*"
to say "Thank you" or "I appreciate you," or even "I love you." Your parents will cherish your words,
and showing your appreciation to them will make *you* feel good, *too*.)

<u>**Life Is A Team Sport**</u>
We All Count On Others to Help Us Through Our Day;
Everyone Is Part of the Team, and Everyone Has a Part to Play

Life Is A Team Sport, and It Takes A Total Team Effort

If you still don't think that life is a team sport, then stop for a minute and think about all the people who help you each and every day. Take a moment to think of all the men and women out there who do their jobs every day, allowing you to be able to do whatever it is that you need to do, and enabling you to do whatever it is that you choose to do.

Let's use a specific example to illustrate this point.

Consider something as simple as a cup of coffee you buy on your way to school or work in the morning…

Someone poured that cup of coffee, and then rang you up at the cash register.

Someone else showed up with that person early that morning to help open up the coffee shop. Both people probably were up much earlier than you.

But simply thinking about those two individuals is rather short-sighted. Let's keep looking deeper and figure out how many other people were involved in something as simple as allowing you to have a cup of coffee in the morning…

Someone ordered the coffee beans and coffee grounds—likely the manager—from the store's original supplier. Someone else owns and runs the store. Several people—in fact, an entire construction crew—helped to physically build the coffee shop in the first place. Another person likely originally purchased the building in which the shop is located, and then leased it out to the company's current owner or manager. A contract attorney had to be present to draft and oversee the signing of the lease documents, as well as the franchising documents from the original company… if the shop is part of a franchise.

Let's look even deeper.

Many weeks and months prior to your enjoying of that precious cup of coffee, someone actually planted the seeds that would eventually bring forth the coffee you would one day drink. Someone else— likely an entire workforce of people—tended the farm on which those seeds were planted, watering and tilling the soil over time. Others likely harvested the raw coffee product, and then passed it on to another department of the farm to be cut, cleaned, processed, and then prepared to ship.

Someone else actually packed the coffee beans, and then passed them on to someone else to load onto a truck. Someone else drove that truck—likely across the country, or even to an airport, where another person then loaded it onto a plane, which was then flown to another destination by a pilot. From there, the coffee packages were unloaded by still more people, who then carried it into a warehouse, where other people proceeded to record the coffee in the warehouse's inventory statement.

Next, that coffee was ready to be shipped; at that point, someone else loaded it onto yet another truck, which yet another person climbed into and then drove across a great distance to help get the coffee to its destination. (Let's not forget all the roads and highways that the truck driver drove along in order to bring that coffee to its newest home… but that adds a whole lot more people than we could possibly fit in the pages of this book. After all, it took thousands of people, and dozens of years to help build all the highways, byways, roads, bridges, and infrastructure of this country.)

Upon its arrival at your local coffee shop, that package of young coffee beans was then unloaded by yet another employee—either bright and early in the morning, or very late at night. That person then unpacked the boxes of coffee, took inventory of their arrival, and then stocked the coffee behind the counter of the store.

And then finally, first thing the next morning, you were ready to walk in to that coffee shop and have someone ground the coffee beans in the coffee machine, and produce a beautiful cup of warm, delicious coffee… which you probably gulped down, half-asleep, without even realizing how many people did their part to help make your day a little better than it otherwise might have been.

~ So, how many people actually were involved in helping to put a hot cup of coffee in your hands? (Oh wait, we forgot all about the cup itself, and all the work and people that were involved in producing, marketing, selling, and shipping that cup… but we'll just estimate that it was a whole lot more than just one person.)

So, back to the original question: how many people actually were involved in helping to put that hot cup of coffee in your hands, and eventually in your belly? Well, none of us can be quite sure of the exact number. But one thing is for certain… It is a whole lot more than just one person.

And it certainly is a whole lot more than just you.

Today, and every day, try to be aware of how many people out there do their part—in some small way— to help make your day a little better.

~

There's no *u* in *humility*… but there had better be *humility* in *you*.

~

Take time to appreciate and thank the people who help you throughout the day.
Take time to appreciate and thank the coffee-shop employee. Take time to thank the staff member.
Take time to appreciate and thank the custodian. Take time to appreciate and thank the bus driver.

Understand that so many people are involved in helping you get through your day, and realize that so many other people are part of the process of helping you to become successful in life.

Never lose sight of the fact that each of us needs a team to help us do everything we wish to do, and that all of us need a team to help us become everything we are capable of becoming.

~

"One guy can't do it by himself,
and it's a matter of recognizing this
and giving others their share of the credit."
~ Archie Manning

~

Be Humble & Share the Stage, Be Grateful & Share the Praise
Being grateful means playing your part in the grand performance that is life,
   But also remembering to share the spotlight and the applause
     With everyone else who's a part of the production as well.

~

Always be aware of the contributions of others.
Always be thankful and grateful to others…
For all that they do… and for all that
They do for you. Be humble.
And always be grateful.

~

~ **A Real Man** ~

A Real Man treats women with respect.
A Real Man always acts like a gentleman.
A Real Man is always polite, courteous, and considerate of women.
A Real Man opens doors, holds umbrellas, and pays honest
Compliments when they are due.

A Real Man always carries himself with class.
A Real Man always speaks respectfully to women.
A Real Man always speaks respectfully *about* women.
A Real Man is never rude or offensive to women. He never uses
Derogatory language, nor does he tolerate others to do so either.

A Real Man listens to women.
A Real Man especially listens to his mother.
A Real Man takes care of his mother and all the women in his life.
A Real Man protects his sister, watches out for his girlfriend,
And takes care of his women friends.

A Real Man respects the strength, courage, and intellect of women.
A Real Man treats women as equals, not as subservient inferiors.
A Real Man treats women as human beings,
Not objects for his own personal gain or pleasure.

A Real Man always does right by the women in his life: whether
They are his family, friends, girlfriend, or wife.
A Real Man always does right by his family.
He is there to be a father to his children,
He sets a good example for the next generation,
And he invests himself fully in his personal relationships.

A Real Man always makes time for what is important,
And he always makes time for *who* is important.
A Real Man helps make the world a more respectful place
By his words and his deeds.
A Real Man helps make the world a safer place for women.
A Real Man makes the world a better place for all people.

A Real Man makes the world a better, safer, more honest,
And more respectful place in which to live.

~

A Real Man respects all women at all times.

~

*"The way you treat women will impact
every other area of your life at some point."*

~ Tony Dungy

32

The Ground Rules for Treating Women

The following is a "Ground Rules for Treating Women: Tip-Sheet. It provides simple and straightforward guidelines for how to show respect and consideration to ladies and women. It is designed to help you to be a finer gentleman, and a better and more genuine man.

**What you must do in order to measure-up,
and to make the cut, as a real and true gentleman…**

~ Be on-time for a date.

~ Call if you are going to be late.

~ Go to the door when you pick a girl up.

~ Call if you say you are going to call.

~ Open doors: car doors, and all doors.

~ Pay for dinner.

~ Pay for dinner… and don't expect anything in return.

~ Pay attention to a woman when she speaks.

~ Listen to a woman when she talks.

~ Make and maintain eye contact… *with her EYES*.

~ Keep your eyes on the woman you are with.

~ Remember what a woman tells you.

~ Know a woman's favorite *anything*.

~ Allow a woman to pick the movie.

~ Allow a woman to pick the music.

~ Share the remote control.

~ Appreciate a woman's presence.

~ Appreciate a woman's contributions.

~ Remember important dates and events.

~ Pay honest compliments.

~ Be careful what you say, and be careful how you say it.

~ Be positive and be thoughtful.

~ Be polite and say nice things.

~ Be tactful and say the right things.

~ Be supportive and be up-lifting.

~ Point out positive goals and encourage ambitious achievements.

~ Be polite and respectful to a woman's family.

~ Be polite and respectful to a woman's friends.

~ Be polite and respectful to a woman in public.

~ Offer your jacket or sweatshirt to a woman when she is cold.

~ Offer your raincoat to a woman when it is raining.

~ Share your umbrella with a woman when it is raining.

~ Offer to carry a woman's bags.

~ Offer your seat to a woman.

~ Go get the car and pull around to the front.

~ Pump the gas for a woman.

~ Stand up when a woman leaves the dinner table.

~ Stand up when a woman stands up, and stand up again when she returns.

~ Be a gentleman, and be a *gentle man*.

~ Never attempt to intimidate a woman.

~ Be tender and delicate, never forceful.

~ Never raise your voice in anger at a woman.

~ Never harm a woman in any way.

~ Never physically hurt a woman.

~ Never, ever, under any circumstances, hit a woman.

   No exceptions. No excuses. Period.

~ Date one woman at a time.

~ Be faithful to the woman in your life.

~ Be a faithful man and find a woman who is faithful to you.

~ Be true to the one woman in your life.

~ Stay true to the one woman in your life.

~ A woman's company is a privilege.

~ A woman's presence is a blessing.

Always be respectful to yourself, toward others, and to the world that you live in.
Always be respectful… especially toward women.

<u>**The Importance of Valentine's Day**</u>
<u>**(One of the Most Important Holidays that There Is)**</u>
Why Valentine's Day Really Matters, & Why It Should Matter to You

What Valentine's Day Really Stands For

Valentine's Day is the holiday where men show their love and appreciation to their significant others and female friends… for having stuck with them, and put up with them, throughout the entirety of football season. (Why do you think it is scheduled for the week after the SuperBowl?)

Whether you are a coach, a player, or even just a fan… make sure you go out of your way to show your thanks and appreciation to the special women in your life. After all, they put up with you (and stuck by you) for the last six months. Show your appreciation, let them know how much they mean to you, and make sure you make it clear that they are special to you in every way. And do not merely express your thanks through only your words alone, but do so with your actions as well. Go above and beyond the bare minimum…exceed expectations and express your appreciation.

~ Valentine's Day matters, and it should matter to you. ~

There is a famous saying in football:
"When your position-coach is happy, *you* are happy. Keep your position-coach happy, and he'll keep you happy. Make him unhappy, however, and he'll make your day miserable."

This is also valuable advice for their future relationships and marriages.
"When your wife is happy, *you* are happy. Make your wife happy, and it will make your life a whole lot easier. Keep your wife happy, and she'll keep you happy. Make her unhappy, however, and she'll make your life miserable."

~ **Valentine's Day matters**. It matters to your spouse and/or significant other, and therefore it should matter to you. If you still don't believe me, take the example of the San Francisco 49ers… whose former owner, Eddie DeBartolo, used to have flower bouquets send to each of the coach's wives every two weeks throughout the entire season. Mr. DeBartolo understand the importance of making the effort to make women happy. He realized that a happy wife makes a happy coach. And a happy coach makes a good, hard-working coach.

---

* Always Remember Valentine's Day *

* Always Remember To Do Something Special On Valentine's Day *

For all you gentlemen out there: be sure to take the time to go out of your way to show your thanks and appreciation to the woman in your life. Do something special for the special woman in your world—whether she is your wife, your fiancée, or your girlfriend. Do something for all the other women in your life as well. Be kind to your siblings, offer compliments to your friends, be thankful to your mothers, and be grateful to your grandmothers.

35

A Profound & Meaningful Quote
What We Really Need: In Football & In Life

What Really Matters This Time of Year (And Really, *Every* Time of Year, For that Matter)
Below is a simple, yet profound quote. Perhaps, as every season of football draws to a close, there might very well be a good parallel between the sport and the game of life. Please take the following quote to heart, and do your best to keep it in mind as you progress through future seasons, situations, and years. Allow it to sink in, and try to hold onto it as you move forward through life. The quote I would like to pass onto you is this:

"The foundation of happiness lies in having three things:
Something to do, someone to love, and something to hope for."
~ The words of philosopher Immanuel Kant ~

We spend the whole season working toward something--Friday nights, Saturday afternoons, etc. We spend the entire season hoping for something--Victories, championships, trophies, rings, etc. Now, it is time to make sure that we go out of our way to show the important people in our lives that we love them, that we care about them, that we respect them, and that we appreciate them.

Another Quick Reminder
* Once again, gentlemen: Once the football season is over, Valentine's Day is next up on the calendar. (Sorry, but there's no more post-season Pro-Bowl to alleviate the sting of Cupid's arrows.) It's time to get back to our families and get on with our marriages. After all: championships are great, but life is all about relationships.

"The two greatest things in life are to love and to be loved."

~ Coach Joe Ehrmann

The Bait Sheet

The Bait Concept: You are the bait that attracts everything else, and everyone else. In other words: the kind of person you are will dictate the kind of people that you attract. The type of man you are, will determine the type of woman you attract also. Be a good person = attract good people. Be a good man = attract a good woman.)

The Important Questions
What characteristics would my ideal woman want in her ideal man?
(What traits would the kind of woman "worth catching" look for in her ideal man?

_____
_____
_____
_____

Which of these traits do I already possess?

_____
_____
_____
_____

Which of these characteristics do I need to work on developing, in order to attract the kind of woman I am looking for?

_____
_____
_____
_____

How can I begin to develop these characteristics? What are some things that I can do to start becoming my ideal woman's _ideal man_?

_____
_____
_____
_____

Who can I learn from, in order to help become a better man? (What good male role-models can I look to for guidance and a good example? What women do I know who I can ask to tell me what they respect in a man, and what they look for in a man?)

_____
_____
_____
_____

Important Women In My Life Sheet

Who are the important women in my life?

What can I respect & admire about them? What can I learn from them?

Who are the most important women in my life?

_____
_____
_____
_____

List each woman's best quality.

_____
_____
_____
_____

List one thing that each of these women is better at, or more capable at, than I am.

_____
_____
_____
_____

What are three things that I respect and admire most about women in general? (Suggestions: The strength to give birth to a child, the courage to raise a child, etc.)

_____
_____
_____
_____

Who are some women in society that I respect? (For example: famous social figures, political figures, professional athletes, musicians, etc.)

_____
_____
_____
_____

List each woman's best quality.

_____
_____
_____
_____

How Do You Know When You See a Good Woman?
(How to Spot a Good Woman When You See Her)

Find A Woman Who Is REAL and Good
We know what it means to be a REAL man… and we know what it takes to be a REAL man as well. We even know what a REAL man looks like, what he talks like, and what acts like. But what about a REAL *woman*? What exactly does a REAL *woman* look like? What does a REAL *woman* talk like, and act like?

How can you tell a REAL woman when you see her? What makes a woman a REAL woman?

First and foremost, a REAL woman is someone who respects herself. She accepts herself, values herself, feels good about herself, and has high expectations for herself. She values others as well as herself, and she sets high standards for herself and for the people she surrounds herself with.

A REAL woman is someone who cares about others and who takes care of herself as well. She respects other people and does right by them, and she is never afraid to be herself in front of anyone, at any time. A REAL woman is respectful and respectable at all times, and she is classy and honorable in all ways.

A REAL woman is someone who respects herself and who can take care of herself. She is someone who has direction and ambition in life. She is someone who is classy, respectable, responsible, and driven to be successful. Above all, a REAL woman is someone who… respects all people, especially herself; she is someone who always does the right thing, and who does her best to live a life that matters.

A REAL woman understands and lives by the creed:

> R~espect all people,
> E~specially yourself.
> A~lways do the right thing.
> L~ive a life that matters.

Be a REAL Man
It takes a king to be with a queen, and it takes a REAL man to be with a REAL woman.
If you want to find a good woman—a respectable, classy, intelligent woman—then you first must become a good man. If you want to find a REAL woman… then you first must become a REAL man.

No matter where you go, and no matter what you do… Always be a REAL Man.
Always think, speak, behave, and act like a REAL Man. Always talk the REAL Man talk… and, more importantly… Always walk the REAL Man walk.
Make sure that you always live out the creed:

> R~espect all people,
> E~specially women.
> A~lways do the right thing.
> L~ive a life that matters.

How Do You Know If You've Found a Good Woman?
The Tests to Tell If You're With the Right Woman

The Tests
1. Find a woman who brings out the best in you.
2. Find a woman who makes you want to be a better man.
3. Find a woman who you would want your future daughter to one-day be just like.

The Test Questions
1. Does she bring out the best in me?
    a. Does she bring out the best in you (Best attitude, decisions, actions, etc.)?

2. Does she make me want to be a better person and a better man?
    a. Does she make you feel like a better man?
    b. Does she make you want to be a better man?

3. If I had a daughter one day… would I want my daughter to be just like her?
    a. This is important, because if you marry and/or have a daughter with a woman, that woman will be the biggest female influence on your daughter… she will have the biggest influence on your daughter's life, and on everything your daughter does and becomes in her life.

Find A Woman Who…
~ Find a woman who makes you proud to be with her
   and who makes you proud to be yourself.

~ Find a woman who makes you proud to be with her,
   not the kind you try to hide from your mother, family, or friends.

~ Find a woman who makes you proud to be yourself:
   the kind of woman who makes you a better man.

Remember the "Right Woman Tests" & Questions To Keep In Mind:
* Does she bring out the best in you (Best attitude, decisions, actions, etc.)?
* Does she make you want to be a better person and a better man?
* If you had a daughter, would you want her to grow up to be just like this woman?

Find a woman who brings out the best in you: the kind of woman who makes you want to be a better man. Find a woman who you would want your future daughter to one-day be just like.

Winning Advice for Winning Over Women – (Guys, This Stuff Is Priceless)
The following is advice designed to help you make a good first-impression, a good next-impression, and a good lasting-impression. It is meant to help you be successful in your dating efforts and in your relationships (and one day, in your marriage). It is meant to help you improve your chances for relational success, and to increase your odds for wining over good women.

This is the best advice I can give you for if you're trying to get a girl to date you, or to be your girlfriend, or one day when the time comes to marry you. There are four things you need to do:

1. **Make her laugh and smile**: A woman has to enjoy being around you and spending time with you. If you're not fun to be with and talk to, then why would she want to?

2. **Make her feel like a lady**: Be a gentleman. Just be polite and courteous; hold the door for her, carry her stuff, etc. Also, don't make sarcastic jokes about her, and don't make fun of her even if it's just in jest. Little things make a big difference with women, and if it's a negative thing they will be hurt by it.
    You had better be a gentleman to the parents too—make sure you look the father in the eye when you shake his hand, and give him a good firm handshake. Don't break eye-contact during the handshake until he does.

3. **Make her feel special**: Make her feel like you treat her better than anyone else could. You have to distinguish yourself from other guys. You have to give her a reason to want to be around you or with you, as opposed to anyone else… If you don't distinguish yourself from other guys, then she doesn't have a reason to choose you.

4. **Be able to dance, and actually like doing it from time to time (if not often)**: Women think guys who don't like to dance are rigid and boring…and if you're boring, then you're not fun to be around. And like I said, if you're not fun to be around, why would she want to be with you?

To Recap…
Make her laugh.
Make her smile; make her happy.
Make her feel special; make her feel like a lady.
Ask her what she wants, ask her what she likes. (About everything)

To Review…
Keep her smiling, and keep her happy.
Keep her feeling special, and keep her feeling unique, lady-like, and wonderful.
Treat her well. Treat her right. Take her the best that you can, each and every day of your life.

She Won't Always Ask You To… But That Doesn't Mean You Can't Always Do It

Say nice things to her: Tell her she looks nice. Tell her she looks beautiful. Tell her she looks lovely and amazing, and amazingly-wonderful. (And really mean it: be truthful.)
She may not always ask you to, but that doesn't mean you can't always say it.

Do nice things for her: Hold the door open for her. Open the car door for her. Help her carry her grocery or shopping bags (all of them). She may not always ask you to, but that doesn't mean you can't always do it.

Say something meaningful to her: Tell her she's special. Tell her you love her. Give her a kiss, and show her she's special. Give her a hug, and show her you love her. Whatever you're thinking, she'd sure like to know and really like to hear. She wants to know that you love her; she wants to know that you care. She may not always ask you to, but that doesn't mean you can't always tell her.

Do something nice to make her feel special: Take her out for a dinner. Take her out to a show. Take her out for a movie. Take her anywhere she'd like to go. She may not always ask you to, but that doesn't mean you can't always do it.

Say nice things to her. Do nice things for her.
Say and do things that are special and meaningful.
She may not always ask you to…
But that doesn't mean you can't always do it.

_____

Go out of your way, to make a woman's day.
By the things that you do, and the words that you say.
She might not always ask you to go out of your way,
To do something kind to help make her day…
But that doesn't mean you can't do it anyway.
So go ahead… go out of your way, to make a woman's day.

Your Ideal Woman:
Writing Assignments & Exercises

1. The Ideal Woman's "Top 10" Exercise
Top 10 Exercise: The 10 Most Important Qualities of a Respectable Woman

* Come up with ten qualities of a respectable women—or even better, of your ideal woman.
* Rank them in order of importance, from 1 to 10. (1 being the first and most important… to 10.)
* Then answer the following questions:

> Why are the qualities you chose so important to you?
> What is the single most important one? Why?
> What are the top three—the three most important?
> What is the one quality you would refuse to be without?
> What is the one quality you would refuse to be without… even if you had the other nine?

2. "The Bait" Exercise
The Bait Concept: You are the bait that attracts everything else, and everyone else. In other words: the kind of person you are will dictate the kind of people that you attract. The type of man you are, will determine the type of woman you attract also. Be a good person = attract good people.)
(Be a good man = attract a good woman.)

The Important Questions
1. What characteristics would my ideal woman want in her ideal man?
   (What traits would the kind of woman "worth catching" look for in her ideal man?
2. Which of these traits do I already possess?
3. Which of these characteristics do I need to work on developing, in order to attract the kind of woman I am looking for?
4. How can I begin to develop these characteristics? What are some things that I can do to start becoming my ideal woman's *ideal man*?
5. Who can I learn from, in order to help become a better man?
   (What good male role-models can I look to for guidance and a good example?)
   (What women do I know who I can ask to tell me what they respect in a man,
   and what they look for in a man?)

3. The Ideal Woman's "Ideal Man" Exercise
Top 10 Exercise: The 10 Most Important Qualities TO a Respectable Woman

* Come up with ten qualities that a respectable women—or even better, your ideal woman—
   would want in *her* ideal *man*—hopefully the future you.
* Rank them in order of importance, from 1 to 10. (1 being the first and most important… to 10.)
* Then consider the following:

1. Go through the list of all 10 traits, and circle the ones you think you need to work on—either a lot, or just a little bit (Remember: there is always room for improvement… You can always get better at something; and you can always be better in some way.)
2. What is the one quality you think you have to work on most?
3. What is one more quality that you really need to work on improving,
    in order to become that Ideal man for whom your Ideal woman is searching?
4. What are some of the qualities that you already possess?
    (It's good to recognize your strengths and to feel good about your good qualities, too!)

The Rules of Attraction: Be the Right Kind of Man,
and You Will Attract the Right Kind of Woman

Rule # 1. Be a good man, and you will attract a good woman.
Rule # 2. Be the right kind of man, and you will attract the right kind of woman.
Rule # 3. Be a REAL man, and you will attract a REAL woman.

Figure out what you want in a woman.
Figure out what she would want in a man.
Do your best to develop those types of qualities.
Do your best to develop all the good qualities you can.

Figure out what you look for in a woman.
Figure out what that type of woman would look for in a man.
Do your best to become that type of man.
Do your best to become the best type of man that you can.

Timely Tips for What to Do & Say
Smart Advice for Playing It Safe

Advice for How to Act & How to Respond…
Things to Think About & Things to Understand

• If your date tells you she's not in the mood, you should… respect her choice and back off.

• If you ask someone out and she turns you down, you should…take it in stride and move on.

• A girl who gets drunk at a party… might simply want to have a good time with her friends.

• A girl who wears tight clothes that show off her body… likes looking pretty, or even sexy.
  But it doesn't mean that she wants to have sex. It doesn't mean that she is a freak or a "ho."
  It doesn't mean that she wants people to cat-call or whistle at her. So don't assume anything.

• If your friends say you're "whipped" because you've been spending a lot of time with your girlfriend…
  tell them you like hanging out with her.

• If you're not sure what your girlfriend wants in a sexual situation… ask.
  If you're not sure… ask. And then listen to what she says.
  Ask. Listen. And then go by what she says.

• If your girlfriend or date doesn't want to get physical, listen to her. Don't push her, and don't force the
  situation. Be polite. Be respectful. Tell her that you understand, and that you respect her decision.
  Listen to your girlfriend. Respect her boundaries. Don't force the situation.
  No one should ever do something they don't feel comfortable doing.
  No one should ever do something they don't want to do.

• If you're not in the mood to hook up and your girlfriend is…tell her straight-up that you're not in the
  mood. Communicate clearly. Be polite, be make sure that she knows you don't feel comfortable.
  You should never do something you don't feel comfortable doing.
  You should never do something you don't want to do.

• If you ever get frustrated with your girlfriend… take some time to cool off and then talk it out.

• If you ever get upset with your girlfriend… take some time to cool off and then talk it out.

• If you ever get angry or annoyed with your girlfriend…take some time to cool off and then talk it out.

• A real man…has the strength to be patient, has the courage to be respectful, has the humility
  to admit when he's wrong, and has the integrity to do the right and respectful thing.

• Practicing safe sex is… both safe and smart.

• Practicing safe sex is… both people's responsibility.

• After a date, if your friends ever want to know if you "got some" … You should respect your date's
  privacy and keep it to yourself. You should have enough respect for her to keep her private matters,
  private. You should have enough respect for yourself to keep your own private matters, private as well.

Always be respectful. Always be genuine. Always be respectable. Always be a gentleman.

~ The Integrity Rules ~

1. Always do the right thing: Always do what is right, always do what is responsible, and always do what is respectable.

2. Always be genuine: Be who you say that you are. Be transparent. Be forthright. Make your words and your deeds match up.

3. Always be yourself: Respect yourself. Be true to yourself. Live by your principles. Be consistent in who you are and in what you believe in, live according to your priorities, and always be true to your values.

4. Always be responsible: Make good decisions, put yourself in good situations, and act appropriately at all times. Do what you're supposed to do; be where you're supposed to be; be on-time, and do what is expected of you when you get there.

5. Always be accountable: Take ownership of your decisions and your actions, and be answerable for their consequences at all times. Assume responsibility for your mistakes, do not blame others; do not make excuses or complain; know when to apologize; know when to grant forgiveness—both to yourself and to others.

6. Always be reliable and dependable: Do what you say you are going to do, and be where you say you are going to be.

7. Always be in control of yourself: Control your emotions, control your compulsions, control your desires, control your behaviors, control your habits, and control your life.

8. Always be honest: Tell the truth at all times, and in its entirety. Be honest with others and be honest with yourself. Be true with others, be true with yourself, and be true with the words you speak. Do not withhold the truth, and do not attempt to stretch it. The truth shall set you free, so long as you respect it.

9. Always be humble: Humility is the ability to see yourself in the correct perspective: to see yourself as you *really are*, not in the way you think you are. Put your personal bias aside, and examine yourself objectively—be able to see yourself for who you really are, both your strengths and weaknesses.

10. Always be respectful: Be respectful to others, be considerate of others, and be civil toward others. Do not make disparaging or hurtful remarks, refrain from gossiping about others; speak all the good you know of others, and speak none of the bad. Give credit where credit is due; praise when appropriate and deserved. Speak ill of no one.

11. Always keep your word: Be true to your word. Keep your promises. Do what you say you are going to do. Value your good name.

12. Always honor your commitments: Do right by others. Fulfill your obligations. Carry out your responsibilities. Follow through on all that you do. Finish what you start.

~

"You can take pride in being an individual of integrity...
People will gravitate to you, seek your counsel, and cherish your friendship."
~ Lou Holtz

<u>The List of *Never's*</u>

If *doing the right thing* and *taking the High Road* are things that you should *always* do… then what are some things in life that you should *never* do? An interesting thought…
Let's explore it further:

1. **Never be afraid of hard work.** It is the only road that leads to progress.
2. **Never make excuses**, and never allow others to make excuses for themselves.
3. **Never accept losing.** Never accept defeat. You may have to deal with defeat at certain points during your life, but always learn from those instances, use them as opportunities to improve yourself, and use them as fuel to motivate you to succeed the next time.
4. **Never accept anything less than your best**.
5. **Never be satisfied** with "good" when "better" is possible.

> *"Don't measure yourself by what you have accomplished,*
> *but by what you should have accomplished with your ability." ~ John Wooden*

6. **Never do something just to take part in it.** Work hard and enjoy your experiences, but never do anything that isn't worthwhile. Never run in a race just to run in it.
Run in it to win.
7. **Never give up.** In anything you do in life, never quit. Keep working hard. Too often, people give up right before their hard work and sacrifice is about to pay off. Keep persevering, keep hoping, and stay positive. Good things will happen.
8. **Never give in.** Do the right thing, at all times. Never compromise with what you know to be right. Even if it costs you… *especially* if it costs you.
9. **Never ask yourself if you've done enough**. Ask yourself *what more* can you do.
Whether it's in your career, your training or athletic career, or you friendships and relationships: there is no such thing as ever doing enough or too much. You can always do more. Never be satisfied with what you've already done. Keep adding to it.
10. **Never compare yourself to someone else's potential**. Focus on your own potential, and do everything you can to work toward achieving it.
11. **Never let someone else or something else dictate your attitude.** Attitude is a choice, and it is entirely your choice. Ultimately, your life is determined by the way you react to each situation that you face. You may not get to choose your circumstances, but you do get to choose how you respond to them.
12. **Never let other people dictate your character.** Be yourself, and dictate your own character. Don't let someone else determine the choices you make and the actions you take. Be yourself, and be confident in yourself.

> *"Be who you are, and be that well." ~ St. Francis de Sales*

13. **Never forget who you are. Never lose sight of who you want to become.**
Never forget where you came from; never lose sight of where you want to go.

~

~ ***Why should you have to settle, when you have the chance to be something special?*** ~

~

~ **The Story of the Mouse Trap** ~

We all live together in this world. Our lives are all connected.
Therefore: what affects one of us… affects all of us.

What Affects One of Us…

One afternoon, a tiny little mouse happened to look through a hole in the local farmhouse's house, where the mouse lived with the rest of his mouse-family. The mouse watched as the farmer and his wife opened a package. "Hmmm…" thought the mouse to himself, "What delicious food might we have here?"

The mouse quickly became distraught, however, when he realized that, of all things, there was no food in the box, but a mousetrap instead. Retreating to the farmyard with a great deal of anxiety, the mouse exclaimed in horror to all the other animals: "There's a mousetrap in the house! There's a mousetrap in the house!"

The chicken—who was the first to see the mouse—clucked and scratched, raised her head and said, "Mr. Mouse, I can tell this is a grave concern to you, but it is of no consequence to me. And so, I cannot be bothered by it."

The mouse turned to the pig and shouted nervously, "There's a mousetrap in the house! There's a mousetrap in the house!" The pig sympathized, but said, "I'm so very sorry, Mr. Mouse, but there is nothing I can do about it but pray. But be assured, you will be in my prayers."

The mouse then turned to the cow and fearfully cried out, "There's a mousetrap in the house! There's a mousetrap in the house!" To this the cow replied, "Gee, Mr. Mouse, that's terribly unfortunate for you. I'm sorry, but it's not any skin off my nose… so why should *I* be worried about it? It's your problem; but good luck with it." So, the mouse returned to the house with his head down and with despair in his heart. He made the long trip back to face the farmer's mousetrap… *alone*.

That very evening, a blood-curdling shriek pierced the night air; it was the sound of a mousetrap catching its prey. Immediately, the farmer's wife rushed to see what had been caught. In the darkness, however, she could not see the venomous snake whose tail had been snagged. And so, she crept closer in order to identify the catch. In a terrible stroke of luck, the snake struck at and bit the farmer's wife.

Coming quickly to her aide, the farmer gathered his wife in his arms and rushed her to the hospital. After a brief stay, the wife would eventually return home, but with a fever and still not at full health. To treat his wife's condition, the farmer turned to the most effective remedy there is for such a diagnosis: fresh chicken soup. And so, the farmer took his trusty hatchet to the farmyard for the soup's main ingredient… and shortly thereafter, the chicken' peaceful life was brought to a swift and bitter end.

But his wife's sickness continued, and so friends and neighbors came to visit and stay with her around the clock. In order to feed the guests, the farmer retrieved his knife and set out to butcher the pig. And thus, the pig's previously-comfortable life suddenly came to an abrupt end.

Unfortunately, however, the farmer's wife did not improve, and she died a few short days later. Such a large number of people gathered for her funeral, though, that the farmer decided to have the cow slaughtered in order to provide enough food for everyone. And so, the cow's life of leisure met its rather untimely demise. At a safe distance, the little mouse looked on as the entire scene of events unfolded. With great sadness in his heart, he had witnessed how the concern of one individual had turned into the downfall of so many others.

We are all involved in this journey called life. So the next time you encounter someone who is facing a problem and think that it doesn't affect you, keep in mind that whenever one of us is threatened, all of us are at risk. Be a man, and be a man of courage. Be willing to take a stand. Stand up for what's right. Stand against what is wrong. Stand up and be a man. Always Remember:

"What affects one directly, affects us all indirectly." ~ Martin Luther King, Jr.

We all live in this world together. We all share the same classrooms, the same hallways, the same locker rooms, and the same schools. We share the same neighborhoods, the same communities, the same cities, and the same world. We are all connected… and what affects one of us… affects all of us.

48

"Stand Up for What You Believe In"
A Courageous Profile of John Carlos & Tommy Smith

Stand Up For What You Believe In

On the night of October 16, 1968, American sprinters Tommie Smith and John Carlos captured the 200-meter gold and bronze medals at the Olympic Games in Mexico City. Smith's time of 19.83 seconds set a new world-record, and Carlos' swift running was fast enough to earn him a place beside his countryman on the medal stand. Despite their performances, however, it would be Smith and Carlos' display following the race that would carve the two men's names into the annals of history.
With racial tensions in America at an alarming high leading up to the Olympics, and with black-American athletes contemplating a boycott of the games, Olympians of all nations were urged not to use the Olympic venue as a platform for making political statements. The stiff and controversial warning was backed by the threat of immediate expulsion from the games.

Immediately following Smith and Carlos' impressive performance in the 200-meters, the two men stepped onto the medal podium in front of a world-wide audience. As the Star-Spangled Banner echoed through Olympic Stadium in Mexico City, Smith and Carlos each pulled on a black glove, bowed their heads, and raised a single fist into the air: a gesture of pride made famous by the Black Panther Party. The poignant salute served as a silent, but strong symbol of protest against the events taking place throughout the United States and around much of the world at the time.

In response to their display, Smith and Carlos were booed harshly by the Mexico City crowd. Merely hours after the record-setting performance, the International Olympic Committee removed the American sprinters from further involvement in the Olympic Games. In the coming days and months, Smith and Carlos would be ridiculed throughout much of the world, and upon returning to their home country, the two—along with their families—would be made the targets of harsh criticism, verbal abuse, and death threats.

History would treat the men much differently, however. As time passed and the initial, emotionally-charged reactions faded, Tommie Smith and John Carlos would gain praise for their controversial stance. While at the time of the incident they were largely scorned and ostracized, Smith and Carlos came to be viewed by many as not only heroic athletes, but also as significant contributors to the Civil Rights Movement in American society.

Over the past 40 years, the two men have been honored repeatedly for their actions and subsequent impacts on the world of sport and in society. Smith and Carlos' famous salute eventually became one of the most symbolic and indelible images of the 20th century. It is forever memorialized in a 20-foot statue that stands on the campus of San Jose State University, the alma mater of both Olympians.

The message is simple, but very important: Always stand up for what you believe in.
Regardless of the consequences, regardless of what other people might think or say, and
regardless of what might happen to you as a result: always stand up for what you believe in.

"No matter what happens, never back down from what you know to be right."
Always do the right thing. Always stand up for what you believe in.

Two Men Took A Stand & Stood Up For What They Believed In
John Carlos and Tommy Smith "Stood Up" for what they believed in.
They literally got up on a podium and stood up for what was important to them.
Both men took a stand: they let the entire world know what they stood for; and, just as importantly, they let the whole world know what they *wouldn't* stand for.

The courage of John Carlos and Tommy Smith serves as a powerful example of conviction and principled living. Their efforts are a testament to their commitment to the ideals of a just society. What both men did was nothing short of inspiring. All of us should be inspired by the stand that these two men took. All of us should learn from the conviction that these two men displayed. All of us should seek to, ourselves, be so inspiring in our own display of commitment and justice.

"The Fictions of Force"
Dispelling the Myths of Violence & Manhood
(To Build Better Men & A Better World)

The Forceful Fictions That Threaten Our World, & What We Can (and Must) Do to Fix Them
There are two great fictions in our society today. There are two big lies, when it comes to violence and manhood, that steer so many young man the wrong way, and then send our world to deeper and darker despair. These two lies—these "Fictions of Force"—revolve around the idea that it is acceptable for a man to be aggressive toward others.

These falsehoods promote the notions of violence and intimidation. They protect the aggressor, rather than looking out for and helping the oppressed. They accept the actions of the perpetrator, rather than addressing the distresses of the victim. The Fictions of Force promote and perpetuate violence. They ensure the prevalence of the hurtful and deadly conditions that exist in our society today, and they perpetuate a more harmful and dangerous world for tomorrow. As a society, as a culture, as a country, and as a world: we must do something to raise awareness about the issue of violence, in order to raise the quality of life for all those who live in this world.

What are these two great lies? What are the "Fictions of Force" that cause so much hurt and heartache in our society? What are the myths of violence and manhood that create so much pain and despair in our world? The only thing that is more important than the answers to these three questions, are the answers that we will offer to address the problems that perplex our world today—to fix the society that steers our men astray, to repair the broken lives of those who have been harmed at the hands of these men along the way, to rebuild the destruction of the innocence of today's children and women, and to restore the hope of a safer and more peaceful future, and the security of a life in a better world.

Fiction #1: Being violent and aggressive towards others makes you a real man.
Fact: The truth is… What defines you as a man is not how rough and tough you can be with others. Being a real man has nothing to do with how violent or aggressive you are be toward others. Being a real man has nothing to do with hurting others. Being hurtful doesn't make you a tough guy. It makes you a thug. Being harmful doesn't get you respect. Being *helpful* does. Being violent and intimidating doesn't make you a man. Being patient and tempered does. Hurting people has nothing to do with being a real man. Your temper does not define you as a man; your *temperance* does. Your ability to keep your composure—to show that you have true power over yourself—makes you a real man. Your ability to remain calm and to stay cool—to demonstrate that you have true power to control yourself and to consider your actions—makes you a *real* man. Your anger does not define you as a man.
Your self-control defines you as a man.

Fiction #2: Being violent and aggressive towards women makes you a real man.
Fact: The truth is… What defines you as a man is not how rough and tough you can be with women. Being a real man has nothing to do with hitting or intimidating a woman. It has to do with being kind and gentle and patient. It has to do with being tender and understanding. Being a real man has nothing to do with controlling or restraining a woman; it has *everything* to do with controlling and restraining yourself. Being hurtful doesn't make you a real man; being *helpful* does. Being harmful doesn't gain you any respect from women; being *heart-felt* does. Your rage does not define you as a man.
Your self-restraint defines you as a man.

51

Don't Be a Thug. Be a MAN.

Thugs never get anything good in life.
Thugs don't get respect.
Thugs don't get jobs.
Thugs don't get women.
What thugs get… is put in prison.

Thugs never go anywhere in life.
Thugs don't go to work.
Thugs don't go to offices.
Thugs don't go to the top of the corporate ladder.

Thugs never end up anywhere good in life.
Thugs never end up with the job.
Thugs never end up with the girl.
Thugs never end up anywhere good in this world.
Thugs end up in jail, in prison, or worse.
Thugs end up with a fate that's as bad as it gets.
Where thugs end up… is inside a casket.

Violence is no joke,
So don't act like a jerk.

Don't Be a Thug. Be a MAN.

Violence only leads to more violence.
What goes around comes around, and thugs always get what they deserve.

"It all comes back around, you're going to get what you deserve.
 Try and test that, and you're bound to get served." ~ Sublime

Thugs eventually get what they deserve.
In the end, they end up getting served.

Violence isn't cool,
So learn to keep your cool.

Don't Be a Thug. Be a MAN.

Get With Good People:
Don't Be a Thug. Be a MAN.
There's no glory in gangs.
There's no victory in violence.
Don't be a thug. But always be a man.
Do the right thing, wherever and whenever you can.

Hang out with good people, make friends with the best.
Stay away from the trouble-makers, don't get caught up in that mess.
Play a sport, and join a team,
Play an instrument, and join a band,
Or play your part, and lend a hand.
But don't be a thug… instead, be a man.

Don't Be a Thug. Be a MAN.
Do the right thing, wherever and whenever you can.
Get with good people, and hang out with the best.
Get away from all trouble, and don't get caught up in that mess.
You only get one life in this world, so make the most of your chance.
Be a teammate, be a band-mate, be a friend… but don't join a gang.
Instead, be a man. Always be a man.

Get with good people.
Don't be a thug; be a man.
There's no glory in gangs.
There's no victory in violence.
Do the right thing, whenever and wherever you can.
Don't be a thug. But always, always, always… Be a Man.

Always Be a MAN.

Always Do
The Right Thing
Make good decisions.
Put yourself in good situations.
Surround yourself with good people.
Be the best man that you can.

Don't be a thug. Be a man.

Don't Be a Thug. Be a MAN.
Stand Up and Stand Tall…
Be a REAL Man!

<u>**Listen Guys: It's Our Problem Too**</u>

Mistreatment of women is not only a *woman's* problem: it is a *man's* problem also.
Not sure what I mean? Think about it...
More than 99% of physical and sexual violence toward women is perpetuated by men.
That means that, as men, we are the source of the problem.

Think About a Football Analogy

To say that violence toward women is a woman's problem—making an analogy to the sport of football—would be like saying that poor blocking is a running back's problem. In reality, bad offensive line play is not a running back's fault: it is an offensive line's fault. The running back does not cause the violence that occurs from being tackled by numerous defenders; he is merely a victim of the circumstances. The cause of the problem lies up front, where the offensive linemen are concerned. The running back is not the cause of the problem; he is merely the one who suffers the effects of that cause.

In much the same way, women are not the cause of the violence that occurs at the hands of men; they are merely the victims of that violence. The source of the problem lies, first and foremost, with men. The bad news is that we, as men, are the main cause of the problem. The good news is that we, as men, are also the potential source of the solution to that problem.

As men, we have created many of the problems that women are forced to deal with. As the perpetuators of these problems, however, we also have the potential to bring about positive change and to create a solution to the issues of our time. We hold in our hands the keys to a better world. It is up to us whether we will use these keys—and both our heads and hearts—to unlock the door to a safer and greater world.

We Have An Obligation to Act Responsibly

As men, we have an incredible obligation to act responsibly and respectfully toward women. Beyond that, we have an incredible opportunity to improve the world in which we live; we have the opportunity to help build a more positive world for ourselves, and to help create a safer culture for the women whom we share this life world with.

As men, the simple fact of the matter is that we have yet to uphold this obligation, and as of yet, we have not taken advantage of our great opportunity. The women we spend our time with, the ladies we share our lives with, and all the women with whom we walk through this world... they all want us to do a better job of being men. They all *need* us to do a better job of being men.

As a gender, we must find a way to do a better job of treating women. We are capable of so much more, we owe so much more, and the women of this world deserve so much more.
To put it simply ... we *can* do better; we *must* do better. We *can be* better; we *must be* better.
Our women need it, our communities need it, our society needs it, and our world needs it.

What affects one of us, affects all of us. That is the nature of a team; that is the nature of a family.
That, whether you like it or not, is the nature of the **Human Team** and the **Human Family**.
And so, if something is affecting one of us, then all of us had better do something about it.

It is no one person's problem; it is no one gender's responsibility. The problem affects all of us—men and women. Therefore, all of us must work to bring an end to the causes of that problem.
We have an obligation to help improve other people's quality of life, and we have an obligation to help improve the quality of our world. The responsibility belongs to us... *all of us.*

54

Respect ALL Women, and Protect ALL Women

Treat *all* women with the utmost respect, not just the ones you want to
or who you think deserve it. Be respectful, thoughtful, and courteous to *all* women.
Stand up and speak up for *all* women, not just the ones you know or care about.
Respect all women, and protect all women. After all, every woman is someone's sister,
someone's daughter, someone's girlfriend someone's wife, or someone's best friend. Even if
that person is not *your* sister, friend, or girlfriend, she is *someone's…*
And she deserves to be respected and protected.

~ Respect women. Protect women. ~

One Day, and Today…

Always remember that, one day… you are going to have a daughter.
Keep in mind that, *today…* you already have a mother, a sister, an aunt, a cousin,
a girlfriend, a best friend, a grandmother, and other women you are fond of.

~

Work to create a better and safer future for your own daughter *one day*.
Do your part to help make a safer and better present
for every woman that you know *today*.

The Main Message:

~ *What affects one of us, affects all of us.* ~

What Male Athletes Can Do
To Take a Stand & Put a Stop to Rape

Athletes as "Men of Strength"

Strength. Sure, it's physical. As an athlete, you know that.
The fastest, fittest, and strongest people in the world are athletes.
They're also some of the most respected. Athletes can do things with their bodies
that make fans' jaws drop. As an athlete, you also know that strength isn't always
measured by the pounds you lift or the miles you run.

Strength is about **character** and **commitment to yourself and others**.
True strength is about what kind of a person you are, and about what kind of a life you live.
It's about how you represent your school, your community, and the world of sports.
It's about having the courage to make the **right choices**.

How Can You as an Athlete Take a Stand Against Rape?

Be a Role Model. Other guys look up to you and respect you. When you're with teammates
and friends, make sure to consistently behave in ways that represent your values.
Don't let anyone pressure you into cat-calling, groping, or taunting.

Define Your Own Manhood. Ask yourself: do messages like *"Never take 'no' for an answer"*
play a role in creating healthy and safe relationships? Decide for yourself what kind of man you
want to be. Decide to be a "good" man. Decide to be a "respectful" and "respectable" man.

Talk it Over with Guys. Most men don't think of rape as being a man's issue. But it is.
So get them thinking about it. How would it feel if a sister, girlfriend, sister, or friend were raped?

Get Educated. Talk to women about how the fear of sexual assault or violence affects their daily
lives. Learn about the issue, so that you can help to support survivors you know, as well as help
to prevent rape by educating other men about the importance of being respectful.

Speak Out. You probably will never see a rape in progress, but you might hear language and see
behavior that put women down and create a threatening environment that can lead to sexual
assault. When your teammate calls a woman a "ho" or a "bitch," tell him that you don't find it
funny or respectful. Tell them it's not "cool," and that you don't respect them for it.

Look Out for Friends. Look out for your friends. Keep an eye on one another. At a party, keep
an eye on anyone that might be behaving in ways that could lead to sexual violence. Watch out
for your group of friends, always stick together, and always protect each other.

Show Your Strength. Use your strength to build others up, not tear them down. Be a positive
person in society, not a destructive force. Help prevent violence, and help create positive change.

6 Things Men Can Do to Prevent Rape

1. Listen and Communicate – Listen to the person you're with. If she says "NO," then you need to STOP. If you're not sure what she wants, ask her. If she says "NO" to sexual contact, or she seems unsure or unwilling, then STOP.

2. Take No for an Answer – Listen to what she says, and don't force her or threaten her to do anything. You may not like her decision, but you need to respect it.

3. Don't Assume You Know What Another Person Wants. Just because a girl wears sexy clothes, drinks, or agrees to be alone with you, doesn't mean she wants to have sex.

4. Don't Cross the Line – If your partner was willing at first, but now doesn't want to go any further, STOP. Don't assume that just because someone has had sex with you before that she is willing to have sex with you again.

5. Don't Be Stupid – If you have sex with someone who is under the influence of alcohol or drugs, passed out, too "out-of-it" to know or agree to what is happening, or unable to say "NO," then it's considered rape.

6. Get Involved – Get involved if you think someone else might be in trouble. If you see someone who could be about to commit rape, or become a victim, step in and help the person who might get hurt. *"Every man is guilty of all the good he didn't do."*

1 out of 6 women in America is a victim of sexual assault.
That's nearly 18 million women.

The Numbers Are Startling: But You Can Help Change Them
Every 2 minutes, someone in America is sexually assaulted.
Almost 50% of rape victims are under the age of 18.
Nearly 85% of victims are under the age of 25.

Have the Courage to Stand Up, and to Speak Up
"Courage is what it takes to stand up and speak."
  ~ Sir Winston Churchill

No … means NO.
Maybe … means NO.
I'm not sure … means NO.

Respect women. Respect their boundaries.
Take no for an answer.

———————————————————

Mothers, sisters, friends, relatives, girlfriends, classmates …

1 out of every 6 women in this country will be the victim of a rape or an attempted rape.
1 out of every 7 women will be victimized before they graduate high school.

Think sexual assault doesn't affect you? Think again.
Rape is a man's issue too.

———————————

How to Help A Friend
What You Can Do To Help a Friend
Who's a Victim, or a Survivor

How can I help someone who has been sexually assaulted?
When a person has been sexually assaulted, your role is to listen, be supportive, to not be judgmental and to provide information if needed. The following list will help you respond most appropriately if someone you know discloses that they have been sexually assaulted. RESPECT.

R.esponsibility
Communicate to the survivor that the assault wasn't their fault, even if the survivor feels they engaged in behavior that may have been risky or foolish. No one ever deserves to be assaulted.

E.mpathy
Believe the survivor. Try to understand what the person has experienced. Think about as time when you felt vulnerable or faced a crisis, and think of what helped you the most. Chances are that it was not a specific conversation that you had, but it was the knowledge and comfort your friends were there for you, believed in you, were on your side and were committed to seeing you through a hard time. These are the things that will help your friend through the healing process.

S.upport
The survivor needs someone to turn to for physical and emotional support and for validation of their experience. If a survivor confides in you this means there is already an element of trust that exists. If they feel supported by you, they may be more likely to seek further assistance. This is crucial for the survivor to begin the recovery process.

P.ower
Survivors of sexual assault feel out of control and powerless. They do not trust their ability to make sound decisions. It is vital for survivors to regain their sense of personal power and belief in their own decision-making. Pushing the survivor into taking actions for which they are not ready may re-victimize them and strip them of their sense of personal power and control. You can best help the survivor by providing options and allowing them to decide. Regardless if you agree with their decision, support their choice.

E.nsure Safety
Survivors often feel unsafe after the assault, both in the immediate aftermath and for any given amount of time after the fact. Encourage them to take appropriate safety measures. This can include changing door and window locks, staying with a friend or have a friend stay with them, and considering transferring jobs or schools, or even moving.

C.omfort
The survivor may experience fear, shock, or any range of emotions and nee immediate comfort from someone they trust. Simply ask the survivor what they need. Don't assume you know what the survivor wants such as physical comfort (like a hug or holding their hand) because that may trigger the assault.

T.reatment
Encourage the survivor to seek medical attention. Encourage the survivor to seek treatment. Encourage the survivor to contact local law enforcement authorities to report the assault. An advocate can provide the information the survivor will need to make this decision. Be patient. Remember, it will take time to not only deal but to heal. Realize that the only person who can decide to reach out for help is the survivor.

Always Take the High Road

Timing Is Everything ~ It's Important To Know When To...
It has been said that timing is everything in life. And so, it would seem important then to always know when to do certain things. An interesting thought. Let's explore it further:

~

In life, it's important not only to know *how* to do the following,
but also *when* to do them as well:

Know when to honest.
Know when to be patient.
Know when to be understanding.
Know when to be forgiving.

Know when to be open to new ideas.
Know when to be open to new people.
Know when to be open to new opportunities.
Know when to be open to new experiences.

Know when to do your best.
Know when to give your all.
Know when to seek perfection.
Know when to strive for excellence.

Know when to believe in yourself.
Know when to have high expectations.
Know when to be optimistic.
Know when to be realistic.

Know when to be resilient.
Know when to keep persevering.
Know when to keep your composure.
Know when to continue achieving.

Know when to be kind.
Know when to be compassionate.
Know when to be fair.
Know when to be considerate.

Know when to be there for others.
Know when to *reach out* to others.
Know when to help out a friend in need.
Know when to help out a stranger in need.

Know when to be respectful to others.
Know when to be tactful in word.
Know when to be hopeful in your thought.
Know when to be helpful in deed.

Know when to keep your head up.
Know when to keep your guard up.
Know when to defend your dignity.
Know when to protect your integrity.

Know when to be true to yourself.
Know when to live by your principles.
Know when to stand up for what you believe in.
Know when to evaluate what you believe in.

Know when to uphold your honor.
Know when to oppose what is wrong.
Know when to stand your ground.
Know when to never back down.

Know when to keep your commitments.
Know when to be responsible.
Know when to keep your word.
Know when to be accountable.

Know when to appreciate all that you have.
Know when to be grateful for all that you've been given.
Know when to make the *most* of everything that you have.
Know when to make the *best* of everything that you have.

Know when to be humble.
Know when to be polite.
Know when to be courteous.
Know when to be unselfish.

Know when to tell the truth.
Know when to *seek* the truth.
Know when to be passionate about life... and …
Know when to do what is right.

~ So, how do you know *when* to do each of these things… ?
Good question. The answer is simple
The answer is … **ALWAYS**.

~ You can never be wrong, if you always do what is right. ~

How Do You Treat Those Who Mistreat You?
The True Test of Your Character

How You Respond to Those Who Mistreat You Is the True Test of Your Character.
How do you treat people who mistreat you? How do you respond to people who are mean to you? How do you act when people are cruel to you? What do you say when people are rude to you?… How do you treat those who mistreat you?

The way you respond to people who mistreat you is the true test of your character.
After all, anyone can be kind when other people are kind to them. Anyone can be polite when others are polite to begin with. However, it is how you respond to people who aren't kind to you that shows your true character

Anyone can do good things for people who do good things for them. Anyone can say nice things about people who speak nice words about them. However, it is how you react to people who try to hurt you, and it is what you say about those who try to slander you, that truly speaks to the quality of your character.

Anyone can show respect to people who show respect to them. However, it is how you respond to people who are mean and hurtful that shows your true character. It is how you treat people who are disrespectful to you, that shows your true level of class.
Anyone can treat people well who first treat them well. However, it is how you treat those who mistreat you, that really shows your true character.
How do *you* treat those who mistreat you?

~

"If you love those who love you, what credit is that to you? Even sinners love those who love them. And if you do good to those who are good to you, what credit is that to you? Even sinners do that. And if you lend to those from whom you expect repayment, what credit is that to you? Even sinners lend to sinners, expecting to be repaid in full. But love your enemies, do good to them." ~ *Luke 6:32-35 (from the Christian Faith Tradition)*

"Love your enemies, do good to those who hate you,
bless those who curse you, pray for those who mistreat you."
~ *Luke 6:27-28 (from the Christian Faith Tradition)*

~

~ Be About Respect ~
Be respectful to all people, no matter who they are or how they treat you.
Be respectful to others… not necessarily because they are respectful;
But because you are.

~

"It's easy to hate, it's harder to love…"
~ *Maino, from the song 'All the Above'*

~ Treat all people with respect, regardless of how they treat you. ~

Violence Is Never the Answer

Violence is never the answer.
Violence is never okay.
It won't make our world any better,
It will only worsen it more, in each and every way.

Violence is never okay. It won't make any of your problems go away.
Instead, it will only increase the hurt and the pain.
It won't do anything to help cure the heartache.

It won't make your hurts disappear,
It will only add to the world more despair.
We don't need any more pain, more hate, or more fear.
We need more patience, more understanding, more care.

Violence doesn't solve anything.
It only makes things worse.
When you respond to violence with more violence,
It only adds more violence to the world.

Violence won't solve anything.
It will only make things worse.
When you fight fire with fire,
All you get is more flames.

We don't need to add fuel to the fire,
What we need is to do better: to be more kind and restrained.
We need to control our tempers,
And not try to create more pain.

Violence is never the answer;
It will make anything better.
Violence won't solve any problems;
And it certainly won't fix anything either.

Violence won't fix our world;
It won't make the world any better.
It will only make matters worse.
We don't need any more hurt in this world.

Let's stop hurting each other. Let's start coming together.
Let's start building a better world with one another.
Let's stop hurting each other, and let's start helping each other instead.
Let's start working together to make this world better.
Let's stop hurting each other. Let's start helping instead.

When you respond to violence with violence, you only put more violence into the world.
We need to stop the vicious cycle. We need to promote understanding and peace. We need to show
some restraint. We need to strive for something better. We need to control ourselves—not each other.
We need to do something better. Violence is never the answer. So let us set out to figure out what is.

Have Something You Can Do, or Someplace You Can Go, to Help You "Cool Off"
A Helpful Analogy about Learning to Cool Off When You Feel You're Getting Hot

Learn to Cool Yourself Off: Take a Jump In the Pool
In the summer time, when it gets really hot outside and you're out at the pool or out to the beach, and it's just sweltering out… what do you do? You need to cool off, right? So, if you are like most people, you're going to run and jump into the pool or the water. When it's getting too hot, and you're starting to overheat… you figure out where the water is and the you go and jump in, don't you? And when you're hot and need to cool off, you dive right into that pool and it's like you're instantly refreshed.

Well, whenever you are really angry, or really upset, and you need to cool off… you need to take the same approach. You have to be able to have someplace that you can go, something that you can do, or someone who you can go to that will help "cool you off." Perhaps it is going for a run, or working out, or going out for a walk; maybe it's calling your mom, or talking to your best friend; maybe it's putting on some music, going for a bike ride, or going for a drive with the windows rolled down… Whatever it is, it's important to have something you can turn to—some "pool" that you can run and jump into—when you feel like you're starting to over-heat and that you need to "cool off."

There are certain people in our lives who we always feel like we can go to when we need to calm down or feel better about ourselves. There are always those people who—no matter how difficult or upsetting are circumstances may be—always seem to put us at ease. Perhaps it is your mother, maybe it is your grandmother; it might be one of your friends; it might be your best friend… Whoever it may be in your own life, the important thing is to know which people have a positive, calming effect on you, so that you can go to them when you are in need of an attitude—or mood—adjustment.

There are always certain people who have a calming, soothing effect on us. It is important to seek out these people when we feel we are getting upset or angry. Such people often can help calm us down and refocus us on what is important, and also on what is good in our lives. These people can help bring us down from our emotional high, help us to calm down and collect ourselves, and help us put things into proper perspective.

Also, there are certain activities that each of us enjoys doing, or that help to calm us down when we could really use it. Maybe it's going to the gym, or heading to the library to relax and read a good book; maybe it's going out to grab a cup of coffee or to get an ice cream… Whatever it may be in your own life, the important thing is to understand which activities help calm you down, cool you off, and help you to feel more positive and pleasant.

Sometimes, there are little things we can do ourselves, that can help us pause for a minute and that can give us the chance to collect ourselves, allowing our emotions to settle down. Sometimes, it might simply be stopping what we are doing and counting to 10. Other times, it might be counting to 100.

The point is that you have to find something, someone, or even someplace that you can go that will help calm you down. You have to have something you can do or someone you can talk to that will take your mind off what is upsetting you at the moment. When you understand what those things, and who those people are, you will be able to seek them out when you are in need of a "chill pill."

Know which people have a calming and soothing effect on you. Know which activities you can do that will help cool you down when you are starting to get upset. Know what techniques you can use to help you keep your composure when you feel yourself starting to get angry. Then, when you find yourself starting to get too hot… you can go to whoever or whatever it is that will help keep you keep your cool. In other words, you can go run and jump into the pool and cool off.

Simple Techniques for Remaining Calm ~ Helpful Ways to Keep Your Composure

Whenever you feel yourself starting to get angry, it is important to find something positive and pleasant to do that can help you remain calm. After all, the easiest way to deal with anger is to prevent it from happening in the first place. Here are a few helpful things you can do to help you keep your cool when you feel yourself starting to heat up…

Techniques for Keeping Your Cool:

~ Count to 10

~ Count to 100

~ Listen to music you like

~ Watch a funny television show or a funny movie

~ Talk to your best friend.

~ Talk to your most laid-back and funny friend.

~ Talk to your mother or your grandmother; talk to your brother or your sister, or whoever it is that puts you at ease when you talk to them.

~ Go for a run

~ Go workout

~ Do pushups

~ Do sit-ups

~ Do forearm curls

~ Squeeze a stress-ball.

~ If you don't have a stress-ball, grab a sponge from the kitchen or the shower, or something else that's squooshy, and use it as a stress-ball.

Find a way to channel your strong emotions in a productive way.
Use your aggression or frustration for positive activities, like working out or running.

"If you are angry, count to ten.
  If you are very angry, count to one hundred."
    ~ Thomas Jefferson

One Play Can Change a Game; One Choice Can Change Your Life ... Choose Wisely

In the sport of football, there may be 80-100 plays in a game. Any single one of those plays has the potential to change the game, or even to decide the final outcome. Over the course of an entire football game, there may only be a handful of plays that ultimately determine who wins and who loses. The important thing to understand is that those plays could happen at any moment. You never know which play might turn the momentum or change the game. It could be this play, it could be the next play. And so, you must always be alert, aware, and ready to meet the moment at hand.

You never know which play is going to decide the outcome of a game, and so you must approach each play—every single snap—as if it were the most important play of the game. You have to be fully poised, fully present in the moment, and ready to think clearly and act decisively. You cannot be over-emotional, otherwise your vision and your judgment will be clouded. You cannot be distracted or disinterested, otherwise your focus and motivation will be lost.

In the game of life, a person may make thousands of choices—some small and some big. And, just like in a football game, where any one play can make the difference; any one decision can make the difference in a person's life. Each choice has the potential to make or break a person's future. And, just like in the game of football, so too in life, you never know when one of those "key moments" is going to happen.

Therefore, you have to approach every decision, and every situation, as if it could be one of the most important choices you will ever make. You never know which decision will impact your life forever, and so you must always be ready—always alert, aware, and prepared to handle each situation with poise.

In order to make the right choices when it counts... when the "game is on the line" ... you have to have your wits about you. You have to be poised and be able to stop and think before you do anything or say anything. Just like with each play in a football game, so too in life must you always be fully poised, fully present in the moment, and ready to think clearly and act intelligently. You can't be overly emotional, otherwise you might make a poor decision out of anger, or put yourself in a poor situation out of frustration. You cannot get distracted, otherwise you might make a bad choice that could cost you in the long-run.

Keep your poise, keep your composure, and keep your wits about you. Be alert and be aware; be ready to think clearly and act intelligently. Always stop to think about what it is you are about to say or do... before you do something that you might regret for a very long time.

In a game of 100 plays, only a handful may ultimately determine the outcome. In a person's lifetime, a lifetime which may involve thousands of choices, only a few of those choices may ultimately decide the way that person's life unfolds. In football and in life, you never know when the "big plays" or the "big decisions" are going to happen. Only one or two of them might end up making the big difference in the grand scheme of things; and you never know which play—or which decision—will end up being one of them. Therefore, you always have to be alert and ready. You always have to be poised and focused, prepared for each play and each decision that you face. You have to approach every single play, and every single decision, as if it were going to be the most important one of your life...
because eventually, one of them will be.

~ Always keep your poise, and always be steady. ~
~ Always be prepared, and always be ready. ~
~ Most importantly: always be thinking. ~

~ **Make the Most of Your Talents** ~

Maximize Your Ability ~ The Parable of the Talents
(A Passage from the Christian tradition: the Gospel of Matthew 25:14-30)

"Again, it will be like a man going on a journey, who called his servants and entrusted his property to them. To one he gave five talents of money, [A talent is a coin—a monetary amount] to another two talents, and to another one talent, each according to his ability. Then he went on his journey. The man who had received the five talents went at once and put his money to work and gained five more. So also, the one with the two talents gained two more. But the man who had received the one talent went off, dug a hole in the ground and hid his master's money.

"After a long time the master of those servants returned and settled accounts with them. The man who had received the five talents brought the other five. 'Master,' he said, 'you entrusted me with five talents. See, I have gained five more.'

"His master replied, 'Well done, good and faithful servant! You have been faithful with a few things; I will put you in charge of many things. Come and share your master's happiness!'

"The man with the two talents also came. 'Master,' he said, 'you entrusted me with two talents; see, I have gained two more.'

"His master replied, 'Well done, good and faithful servant! You have been faithful with a few things; I will put you in charge of many things. Come and share your master's happiness!'

"Then the man who had received the one talent came. 'Master,' he said, 'I knew that you are a hard man, harvesting where you have not sown and gathering where you have not scattered seed. So I was afraid and went out and hid your talent in the ground. See, here is what belongs to you.'

"His master replied, 'You wicked, lazy servant! So you knew that I harvest where I have not sown and gather where I have not scattered seed? Well then, you should have put my money on deposit with the bankers, so that when I returned I would have received it back with interest.

"'Take the talent from him and give it to the one who has the ten talents. For everyone who has will be given more, and he will have an abundance. Whoever does not have, even what he has will be taken from him. And throw that worthless servant outside, into the darkness, where there will be weeping and gnashing of teeth.'"

~

The Main Message
Make the most of your talents and abilities.
If you are capable of greatness, then don't settle for anything less.
~
"From everyone to whom much has been given, much will be required; and from the one to whom much has been entrusted, even more will be demanded."

~ Luke 12:48 (From the Christian Faith Tradition)

Excellence & Personal Pride
Positive Pride: The Good Kind of Pride

Excellence is a positive form of personal pride. It is the good type of pride: the kind that is focused on making the most of your talent and opportunities; the kind that is focused on helping you reach your absolute full potential. This type of pride involves always striving to do your best and to do your all; it involves always giving your best to everything you do, and always giving your all in every way.

~ Excellence means always…

> ~ Doing your best.
> ~ Doing your all.
> ~ Giving your best.
> ~ Giving your all.

~ Excellence means always…

> ~ Striving to be first-rate in anything and everything you do.
> ~ Striving to be first-rate in who you are and who you become as a person.
> ~ Striving to give your greatest effort to life and the way you live it.
> ~ Striving to reach your greatest potential at all times, and in all ways.

~ Excellence means…
> ~ *Giving your all* to accomplish *all* that you are capable of accomplishing.
> ~ *Giving your all* to become *all* that you are capable of becoming.

~

**"The best kind of pride is that which compels a person
to do his very best work – even when no one is watching."**
~ Anonymous

~

~

"A champion is someone who gives his best all the time."
~ Mike Kryzewski

You Are Not In This World for Free: You Are Here On Scholarship

You are not in this world for free; you don't get to just live here without paying rent or earning your stay. You aren't just here to take care of yourself and have as much fun as you possibly can and that's it. Quite the contrary: you are basically here on a *scholarship*: you get to live and experience all this world has to offer, but in exchange, you have to put in the work. That is the bargain of being alive.

Just like when you are on an athletic scholarship—where you have to go to practices, you have to go to meetings, you have to participate in early-morning workouts, you have to be responsible and accountable, you have to have class, you have to represent your "program" and your "family" well, you have to be a leader, and you have to be a builder and an encourager of others—so too in life, must you learn to do all the things that are expected of you… and to do them all to the best of your ability, at all times, and in all ways. You must honor your scholarship. You must uphold your end of the bargain.

Whether you are on a scholarship in school, or on a 'scholarship' in life, the same fact remains true… You have a great opportunity, but it doesn't come without a price.
In exchange for all you get to experience, you owe it to the rest of the world to give your best, to do your best, to help others do their best, and to be a blessing to the lives of others in the process… and you are expected to uphold your end of the bargain.
Otherwise, you are practically stealing.

"Any person who does not fully believe in himself and fully utilize his ability is literally stealing from himself, his loved ones, and in the process – because of reduced productivity – is also stealing from society."

~ D. W. Rutledge

Any person who does not work to develop his talents and take advantage of his opportunities, robs himself of the wonderful experience of realizing what he is fully capable of becoming. What is even worse, he robs the lives of those around him and the world in which he lives, of all the wonderful and meaningful contributions he is capable of making. Such a man is stealing from everyone, everywhere.

In another sense, the person who neglects his talents and opportunities is like a gift-giver who wraps presents for others, but then never actually gives them. A gift to the world which forever remains unopened, is not a gift at all, but a travesty. A man's potential which forever remains untapped, is not a blessing at all, but a tragedy.

~

*"If you don't use your talent, then you're stealing.
You're stealing from yourself, you're stealing from this world,
and you're stealing from your Creator."*

~ Herman Edwards

"To give anything less than your best is to sacrifice the gift."

~ Steve Prefontaine

Maximize Your Impact In This Lifetime:
Strive to Do Absolutely Everything You Are Capable of Doing In This World

"What did you do with your life? What did you do for the lives of others? Those are two of the important questions that you'll be asked when you leave this world.

~ Make the most of your abilities and opportunities. Become everything you were meant to become. Accomplish everything you were meant to accomplish.

~ Make the most of your abilities and opportunities to impact the lives of others. Do everything you can to positively affect other peoples' lives. Do everything you can to improve other peoples' lives. Do everything you can to help raise other peoples' quality of life. Make the most of every chance you have to give hope and encouragement to others. Do your best to set a good example for others, and do your best to be a positive role model for others.

~ Do your best to reach your full potential, and do your best to help others reach their full potential as well. Strive to make the most of your life, and strive to help others to make the most of their lives as well.

~

Do all you can do, and do all that you can do for others.
Do the best that you can do, and do the most that you can do for others.

~

You only get one life, you only get one opportunity to live it, and you only get one chance to do the absolute most that you can in it. You have to do everything you can to get the most bang for your buck. Don't just be satisfied with doing a little, or even with doing a lot. Strive to **do absolutely everything you are capable of doing in this world**. Don't just try to make a difference in your own life or in just one other person's life; try to make a difference in as many people's lives as you can.

~

~ Paid In Full ~
Your life is not *your* life: it's merely on loan to you.
And, at the end of it—when you go to settle your debts—you are going to be expected to pay it back with interest. In other words: you had better have something to show for your time in this world. You had better be able to point to the contributions you made during your lifetime. You had better be able to speak of more than just what you did for yourself and in your own life. You had better be able to say that you took all the talents and opportunities that you were originally given, and that you maximized them and developed them as best as you could. You had better be able to say that,
whatever you were loaned in the beginning, you have paid back with interest.
When you sign your name on the final page of your life,
you had better be able to follow it up with the words:
"Paid In Full."

I CAN. I WILL.
Why I Can & Will Accomplish My Goals & Succeed In Life

Choose three goals for yourself: Pick one goal for your academics, pick one goal for your sports career, and pick one goal for your future or your business career. For each goal, decide what you want to accomplish, and then decide when you want to accomplish it (this week, this year, next season, by the time you graduate, etc.).

Next, think about why you CAN in fact accomplish your goal. (What skills and talents do you possess? What qualities and character traits will help make you a success?) Then, after you write the reasons why you CAN achieve your goal, write the words: "I CAN!" (in big, bold letters!)

Finally: Make a commitment to accomplish your goal and achieve your dreams.
Write down one reason why you WILL succeed and achieve your dream. (Write something like: "I WILL succeed because I won't give up until I do." OR: "I WILL succeed because I will work hard to be successful.") Then, after you write the reason why you WILL succeed... write the words: "I WILL!" (Write it in big, bold letters... with at least 1 exclamation point!)

GOAL (Here's What I Want to Do:)	I CAN Do It (and Here's How:)	I WILL Do It (and Here's Why:)
1.		
2.		
3.		

Graduation Commitment

I Commit To Making the Most of My Education.

I Commit to Crossing the Educational "Goal Line" and Earning My College Degree.

* I will do everything in my power to go to school, stay in school, and graduate from school.

* I will do everything in my power to go to college, stay in college, and graduate from college.

I CAN go to college. I WILL go to college. I CAN graduate from college.

I WILL Graduate from College.

Name _____

Signature _____   Date _____

__Graduation Commitment__

I Commit To My Education: I commit to make every effort
To attend high school, to graduate from high school,
To attend college, and to graduate from college.

Name _____

Signature _____   Date _____

Operation Goal Line – Group Commitment

I commit to do everything I can to graduate from high school,
To go to college, and to graduate from college.

I commit to do everything I can to help & encourage
My teammates to graduate from high school,
Go to college, and graduate from college.

Signatures:

_____   _____

_____   _____

_____   _____

_____   _____

_____   _____

_____   _____

_____   _____

_____   _____

_____   _____

_____   _____

_____   _____

Operation Goal Line – Group Commitment

I commit to do everything I can to graduate from high school,
To go to college, and to graduate from college.

I commit to do everything I can to help & encourage
My teammates to graduate from high school,
Go to college, and graduate from college.

Signatures:

_____   _____

_____   _____

_____   _____

_____   _____

_____   _____

_____   _____

_____   _____

_____   _____

_____   _____

_____   _____

_____   _____

_____   _____

Winners Find A Way!

Don't Find an Excuse; Instead Find a Way!

Losers Find an Excuse

Losers find an excuse to miss practice.

Losers find an excuse to miss a training session.

Losers find an excuse to be late, or not show up at all.

Losers find an excuse not to work hard.

Losers find an excuse not to do their best.

Losers find an excuse for why they did not give their all.

Losers find an excuse for why they let other people down.

Winners Find a Way

Winners FIND A WAY to make it to practice.

Winners FIND A WAY to make it to a training session.

Winners FIND A WAY to be on time, or early.

Winners FIND A WAY to work hard, and to continue to work hard.

Winners FIND A WAY to do their best.

Winners FIND A WAY to give their all.

Winners FIND A WAY to make themselves and others proud.

… WINNERS FIND A WAY!

"If you really want to do something, you will find a way.
   If you don't, you will find an excuse."
      ~ *Anonymous*

"Winners find a way…
   Never give up!
      Find a way…
         Because that's what winners do!"
            ~ *from the movie, Surf's Up*

"My Philosophy Of Winning"
by George Allen, Hall of Fame Coach

To Be Successful…
To be successful, you must win.
To win, you must WORK HARD.

You must DEDICATE yourself to a far-reaching goal…and sacrifice to reach it.
You must ENJOY what you do… be enthused with your activities,
in love with the idea of winning.

You must REACH BEYOND your abilities.
Recognize that no talent, without hard work, can make you a winner.
You must BE HONEST with yourself—and with others…
There is no easy way to success.

You must treat your body with respect…
disciplining yourself into SUPERB PHYSICAL CONDITION.
You must BE LOYAL… to yourself, to your ideals,
and to your team or family.

You must become a LEADER, first leading yourself,
and then leading others by your example.
You must have a complete MENTAL COMMITMENT,
overcoming all defeats, relentlessly pursuing total victory.

You must consider winning as essential as eating and sleeping.
You must consider success the heartbeat of life.

"The difference between a successful person and others
   is not a lack of strength, not a lack of knowledge,
     but rather in a lack of will." ~ Vince Lombardi

Competition Drives Us To Our Full Potential

It is the competition to win – the drive to be the best –
that enables us to achieve our full potential.
Compete… Compete… Compete.

~ Always Compete ~

What Does It Take
To Achieve Success ?

It takes discipline.
It takes desire.
It takes motivation.
It takes determination.

It takes drive.
It takes ambition.
It takes commitment.
It takes conviction.

It takes passion.
It takes purpose.
It takes enthusiasm.
It takes courage.

It takes toughness.
It takes persistence.
It takes resilience.
It takes endurance.

It takes your all.
It takes your best…
It takes hard work.
To achieve success.

~

What does it take to achieve success? What does it take to be the best?
The answer is simple... The answer is: *everything*.
If you want to achieve success, if you want to be your very best,
Then you have to give everything you've got in life.

~

"What does it take to be the best? **Everything**.
And *everything* is up to you."

~ Emmitt Smith ~

Four Steps To Achieving Success

Step One:
VISUALIZE

You must first determine your definition of success: What does success mean to you?
What you are trying to achieve, what mission are you going to set for yourself?
What does the final outcome or the finished product look like in your eyes?
~ **Have a Vision**: See what is possible for you to do. See what is possible for you to become.
Figure out exactly what you want. Determine your intended destination.

Step Two:
CONCEPTUALIZE

Once you have established your objective, you must then determine what it will take to achieve
success: How will you work toward accomplishing your objective? What steps will you take?
How long will you need to do it? What is your plan of attack going to be?
~ **Create a Plan of Attack:** Put together the plan, determine what steps you will need to take in
order to achieve the end-goal of that plan, understand what you will have to go through in order
to effectively navigate your pursuit of success. Create a plan of attack to reach your goals,
then prepare to attack every step of that plan with a strong and determined sense of purpose.
Get ready to work toward accomplishing your goals.

Step Three:
ACTUALIZE

Once you have established a plan of attack, you must begin to actively attack the plan.
You must roll up your sleeves, get to work and get down to business, and make
success happen. After all, success won't just come to you; you must go to it.
~ **Implement the Plan**: Put the plan into action. Breathe life into your mission by beginning to
walk the walk of success. Begin living out your mission by taking each and every step—one
focused and determined step at a time—along your pathway to success. You have already
created the plan of attack, now it is time to attack the plan.
Actualizing means taking what you *plan* to do… and ***actually doing it***.

Step Four:
REALIZE

Once you have worked and labored in the direction of achieving your goals,
you must follow through and persevere to the very end of the course you set for yourself.
You must finish the job. You must do everything in your power to take your original dream—
that initial vision—and turn it from a fantasy into a reality. You must do everything you possibly
can to bring your ultimate mission to fruition.
~ **Finish**: Finish the plan. See it through. Bring the mission to fruition.
No matter how long it takes, no matter how hard it gets, and no matter difficult it becomes…
Finish the job. Take the final steps toward your ultimate destination.
Bring the dream to life. Focus on the task at hand, and finish what you began.
Transform your original dream into reality. Make it happen, and make it real.

Visualize. Conceptualize. Actualize.

REALIZE.

~ __Successful People__ ~

Successful people set goals for themselves.
Then they establish a clear and logical plan to achieve those goals;
Then they work hard and persist, until they accomplish their objective.
They persevere until they bring their mission to full fruition.

~

~ __Accomplish Your Mission__ ~

You have to work hard and keep working hard;
You have to persevere and keep believing;
You have to resist the temptation to quit and to give in;
You have to continue to press on until finally,
At long last, you have accomplished your mission.

~

**Ambitious people set goals. Passionate people work toward those goals.
Committed people—*successful people*—finish the job and accomplish those goals.**

Success In Life Depends On Determination

Success in life depends much less on a person's outer circumstances than it does on his inner determination. Very often, we look for what we believe is the "ideal" situation to propel us toward success. We grow discouraged when that situation doesn't present itself right away, and we tend to get frustrated when our accomplishments don't show up as quickly as we'd like them to. Often times, we fail to realize that success is not something to be granted us, but rather, something that must be consistently and persistently worked for. **The key ingredient for success is not having the perfect situation, but instead, having a perfectly-determined attitude with which to face the current situation.** No set of circumstances, no matter how difficult, is any match for a determined attitude and a relentless effort.

"There is no chance, no destiny, no fate, that can hinder
or control the firm resolve of a determined soul."

~ Ella Wheeler Wilcox ~

Stay Committed, Stay Persistent, and Finish the Job

A job that is worth doing deserves your full attention, your full ability, and your full commitment. It also deserves your full determination and commitment to finish it. If you start something, make sure you see it through to its completion. This is never an easy task, but you must stay committed, through the good times and the bad. Some people give up just before they are about to achieve their goals; don't be one of those people.
"Commitment in the face of conflict produces character."
Stay committed. Finish the job. See it through.
Do what you set out to do.

"See It Through and Never Quit"

Whether you wish to win just a little bit,
Or you hope to conquer life and be a great hit,
If you wish to do whatever it is that you see fit,
Then see it through and never quit!

Some call it determination, and some call it grit.
Although it means the same, howe'er it be writ.
If you wish to do whatever it is that you see fit,
Then see it through and never quit!

If you've found something to be done, then go out today and do it.
If you know that it can be done, then go ahead and prove it.
But don't you stop and don't you sit; and don't you rest—not for just one bit.
See it through… and never quit!

"It is the surmounting of difficulties that makes heroes."

~ Louis Kossuth ~

Choose Greatness: Decide To Be Great!

~ Everyone Can Be Great ~
Within each of us lies the potential for greatness.
The opportunities are unlimited and the possibilities are endless.
Do not settle for being mediocre; do not settle for merely being good.
Desire to be something special. Endeavor to reach the heights of greatness.
Resolve to become someone unique and extraordinary.
Do everything you are capable of doing, and strive to
become everything you are capable of becoming.
Don't just try to be good… Dare to be great.

~ Choose Greatness ~
Just like with success, *greatness* is also a choice.
More importantly—just like success—greatness is *your* choice to make.
So how does one choose greatness? Simple: A person chooses greatness by choosing
to give his very best at all times, and to do his very best in all ways. A person chooses to become
great by giving his greatest efforts to everything he does. He chooses to become great by striving
to do his greatest work with anything and everything that he does.

Greatness is simply a matter of commitment.
Choosing greatness is simply a matter of making a commitment to be great.
Making a commitment is simply a matter of choosing to do so.
"A man can be as great as he wants to be."
~ Vince Lombardi ~
~
"A man can do just about anything that he really wants to and makes up his mind to do.
We are capable of greater things than we realize." *~ Norman Vincent Peale*

~ Are You Willing to Become Great? ~
Your character is a combination of your thoughts, your habits, and your priorities.
It determines the choices you make, and the choices you make determine who you become.
Who you become will determine what you accomplish.
~ Are you willing to do what it takes to become special? ~
~ Are you willing to do what it takes to become great? ~

The Seed of Greatness Lies In Us All
There exists a divine spark inside all of us;
it is up to us to fan the flames and stoke the fire.
"Each one of us is born with a seed of greatness,
and it is our responsibility to nurture it and make it grow."
~ Edie Raether ~

You have the potential for greatness!

A Call to Greatness

There Are Two Types of People In This World... Which Type of Person Are You?

There are two types of people in this world: there are those who live day-to-day and who are just trying to get by—the ones whose only goal is simply to make it to tomorrow. Then, there are those who have some great hope for their lives—something grand and worthwhile that they want to accomplish... some unique and special thing that they want to do with their lives—the ones who realize that there is something special the world needs them to do. **"Great hopes make great men."** ~ Thomas Fuller

The world calls each of us to greatness. Unfortunately, not everyone is able to hear that call, and not everyone who hears it is actually willing to answer it. Those people who have great hopes and high expectations create an overwhelming purpose in their lives. They wake up each and every day, ready and willing to battle through any adversity that comes their way, flexible enough to adjust to any situation that may arise, open to change and prepared to embrace new opportunities for growth, and ready to enjoy the many blessings that life has to offer.

Those **strong souls are motivated by something greater than mediocrity**; they live for something far beyond what the average person would be satisfied with. Such people strive to reach onward and upward toward some great and worthy purpose. These inspiring individuals are made great by their lofty aspirations and their unyielding determination. Their lives are made special by the pursuit of, and ultimately, the bringing to fruition of the most extraordinary of hopes.

There are two types of people in this world: there are those who are content to live day-to-day, and those who are spurred on by something of greater significance. There are those who are satisfied merely with trying to get by, and there are those who have a burning desire to do something special—something *extraordinary*—with their lives.

So...
Which type of person are *you*?
Do you want to do "big things?"
Do you want to accomplish "great things?"

How good do you want to be?
More importantly, how GREAT do you want to be?

It is the nature of man to rise to greatness if greatness is expected of him.
It is the destiny of man to rise to greatness if he expects greatness of himself.

The REAL Keys to Success

If you are willing to make a commitment to something worthwhile, if you are willing to make the necessary sacrifices, if you are willing to work hard—because nothing worthwhile in life will come easily—if you surround yourself with good people, if you put yourself in good situations, if you make good decisions, if you persevere through adversity, if you persist through the hard times of life, if you will give your all for a worthy cause, and if you will never settle for anything less than your absolute best…

then you will accomplish what you set out to do in this world, you will get to where you want to go in this life, and you will have found the keys that will unlock the door to real and lasting success.

Life and Football

My experience with coaching has taught me that, in many ways, football is just a game. Yet, in many ways, football also is far more than a game. And, at the same time, it is important to understand that life, itself, is also a game of sorts, and that the same things that will allow a person to be successful in the game of football will also enable him to be successful in the game of life…

~ If you live by your principles and stand up for what you believe in…
~ If you work hard and dedicate yourself…
~ If you commit yourself to excellence and continuously pursue improvement in
     everything you do…
~ If you make the sacrifices necessary to help put you in the best position to accomplish
     your goals…
~ If you remain humble through the successful times and stay positive during the
     challenging ones…
~ If you persevere through adversity and refuse to give up no matter how difficult the
     circumstances become…
~ If you respect yourself and others and treat everyone with compassion and dignity…
~ If you keep your poise and never lose your composure…
~ If you keep everything in your life in proper perspective…
~ And if you surround yourself with good people who can help you make it through times
     of trial and who can help you to become the person you are capable of becoming…

Then you are going to have success in almost everything you do.
More importantly, if you learn to do all those things, you are going to end up living a life of meaning and value as well.

Competitive sports can teach you how to *practice* with purpose and how to *play* with purpose. If you understand that the very same lessons that apply to the game, also apply to the game of life, then the world of sports can teach you one very lasting and important lesson as well: it can teach you how to *live* with purpose.

~

~ Practice with purpose. Play with purpose. Live with purpose. ~

~

84

How Do You Define Success:
Success In the Game of Life Can Be Defined As...

~ Doing all you can to make the absolute most of all your talents and abilities, achieving everything that you are capable of achieving, and helping others to do all they can to reach their fullest potential: Success means reaching your absolute potential—not just improving a little bit, but improving as much as you possibly can improve, based on your own individual talents and abilities.

~ Keeping your priorities in proper order: Success means having the right priorities, and more importantly, success means making sure your life corresponds to those priorities at every moment, and in every way... each day, every day, every time, and all the time.

~ Always living by your principles: Success means having solid and noble principles, and more importantly, success means always living by your principles in everything and anything you do.

~ Always doing the right thing: Success means treating all people with respect and dignity, always carrying yourself with the utmost class, having integrity in every way, being honorable at all times and in all things, being honest and sincere in all of your dealings, being respectful at all times and being respectable in all ways, being responsible for yourself and being accountable to others, standing up for what you believe in and for what is right, attacking injustice and standing against what is wrong, and ultimately for doing all you possibly can to reach your absolute full potential in every regard.

Priorities & "Potato Chips"

There are a lot of things in life that are important. There are a lot of people, principles, goals, and pursuits that are worth investing your time and attention into. There are also a lot of things that *aren't really* important—things that people often get caught up in, or distracted by, and end up missing out on the most important aspects of life.

The important things—and the important people—are like the "meat and potatoes" of life: they are the substance, the main course, the good stuff. All the other things—the things like your clothes, the car you drive, how many points you score, how many people know your name, etc.—all these things are like the "potato chips" of life: they may taste good, but they won't fill you up. They won't *fulfill* you.

They will just leave you hungry for something more… something better, something more meaningful. In order to "get your fill" of the good things in life, you first have to understand what aspects are indeed the "meat and potatoes," and what things are just the "potato *chips*."

Important Questions to Help You Determine the Important Things In Life
What are the most important things in your life? (Or, at least, what *should* they be)?

_____
_____
_____
_____
_____

Pick 4 of the most important aspects of your life. Write them down, and then think about what they each mean. What are your "priorities?" What do each of these things mean to you?

1.
_____
_____
_____

2.
_____
_____
_____
_____

3.
_____
_____
_____
_____

4.
_____
_____
_____
_____

What are some things in life that can be called "Potato Chips?"
(What are the things that people often get caught up in, that really, in the end don't matter a whole lot?)

_____
_____
_____
_____

Why do you think it's important to pursue *meaningful* goals? (Why is it important to eat the "meat and potatoes?") Why do you think it's important to invest your time and your efforts into the things—and the people—that matter most in life?

_____
_____
_____
_____
_____

Do you think it's important to build meaningful friendships and relationships? Why?
Do you think the quality of your friendships will help to improve the quality of your life? How could it?

_____
_____
_____
_____
_____

Write a Letter: Tell Someone Else What Really Matters, and What Really Doesn't
Imagine you were going to write a letter to your younger brother or sister…
(Or imagine you were going to write a letter to your future son or daughter…)
Imagine that you are going to tell them all about the important things in life: the things that *really* matter.
Write your letter to them, and tell them:

       1. Why it's important to have priorities in life.
       2. Why it's important to have the *right* priorities in life.
       3. What things *really* matter—what things *really are important*.
       4. What things *don't really matter* that much, no matter what society or other people say.

As you write your letter, keep in mind that the advice you give can help shape another person's life.
What you tell them, and what you suggest, will help them to make decisions about their life and their future. So think long and hard about what's really important, and what isn't—about what really matters, and what really doesn't. Give good advice: advice that's worth following; advice that *you* can follow, too.

_____
_____
_____
_____
_____
_____
_____
_____
_____
_____

Two Simple Rules for Friendship
Important Ideas that Every Friend Should Remember

Rule #1: Be the best friend that you can be.
Be the best friend that you can be. Strive to act your best, and you will bring out the best in others. Be as good a person and as good a friend to others as you can be, and you will attract good people and good friends more often than not. Try to be the right kind of person, and you will find that the right kind of people will gravitate toward you.

Rule #2: Be forgiving of others.
Be forgiving of others. Remember that no one is perfect: not others, and certainly not you. That simply is part of the nature of life. Rather than spending your time being judgmental or getting frustrated with others, learn to hope for the best from them, but not to require it as a pre-requisite for your own satisfaction. Expect a great deal from yourself, and strive to live up to your own personal lofty expectations. Look for the best in others, hope for the best *from* others, but do not expect other people to be perfect. They simply are not, and neither are you. Keep that in mind.

~ Exercise patience and forgiveness accordingly.

Learn to Say "I'm Sorry"
Offering a heartfelt apology to someone is the opposite of making an excuse. Learning to say "I'm sorry" is part of being truly accountable. In order to do this, one must know when one is wrong and be willingly ready to admit to it. Owning up to a mistake or ill deed is often very difficult. Apologizing for your words and actions always takes tremendous amounts of courage. It also involves swallowing your pride and giving way to someone else's concerns and welfare; not always an easy task to perform.

Two Simple Words that Make a World of Difference
Learning to tell someone that you are truly and authentically sorry is the first step in repairing your relationships and in getting yourself back on the right track. Learning to ask that person for forgiveness is the second step.

Apologizing to and asking forgiveness of someone often seems much more difficult than it really is. Once you have figured out how honestly to do both, you will find that your relationships, and ultimately your life, become much more positive and rewarding. Your interactions will lend themselves to more trust, both from yourself and the people to whom you relate.

Learn to realize when you have said or done something wrong to another person. Learn to humble yourself and swallow your pride. By teaching yourself to apologize and ask forgiveness, you will make the people in your life happy, and yourself even happier.

~

**"It takes a strong person to say sorry,
and an ever stronger person to forgive."**

~ Anonymous

A Roadmap For Your Life

It is always important to have a roadmap for your life—some idea of where you are trying to go, and of what you are trying to accomplish during your time in this world. Every now and then, it's good to do a quick self-assessment to make sure that you're on the right track and that you're headed in the right direction. Below are a few simple questions worth keeping in mind as you go through life-they are the *Who*, *What*, *Where*, *Why*, and *How* that we should all try to answer...and the *When* is *always*: *Now*.

Who: Who are you, and who are you trying to become? Whom do you want to be when you grow up? Who do you want to emulate, or try to be like, in life—who are your role models? What kind of person do you want to become... and how will you develop yourself into that type of individual?

What: What do you want to accomplish in your life? What do you want to achieve? What goals are you setting for yourself... and what are you going to do to achieve them? Are you doing it? Have you started working at it yet? Are you doing the best that you can? Are you making the most of the talents and opportunities given to you?

Where: Where are you going in life?... Where is that final destination—that future vision of your life— that you are working toward? Who is that "Ideal You"—that future version of *yourself* who you are working to become?

Why: Why are you here?... Why were you put on this earth? What were you born to do? What is your purpose... and how will you carry out your life's purpose?

How: How do you want to be remembered? ... How do you want to impact other people's lives and the world around you? Are you living in such a way, that your legacy will be, what you *want* it to be?

All these questions can be posed s *to* you, but I can't answer any of them *for* you. That part is up to you...and you can only do it by <u>living out</u> your answers... Through the decisions that you make and through the actions that you take.

Choose Well ... and, more importantly... **LIVE** Well.

Some Important Questions To Consider In Life
What will you do with your life? Will you make the most of it?
Will you make the most of your time in this world?
What will your life's message be? What will you stand for? What will you make your life speak for?
What will your legacy be? How will you be remembered? What will people say about you in the end?

All these questions may be posed to you; however, none of them can be answered for you.
The way you live your life and the legacy that you leave behind you in this world, are completely up to you to decide. Only you can determine the way you live your life and the legacy you leave behind.

Your life is what you make it. The power to live your best life and leave your best legacy is entirely in your hands. What will you do with that amazing power? The opportunity to live honorably and to leave a noble legacy is entirely up to you. What will you do with that wonderful opportunity?

Think carefully and choose wisely. Then go out and live well and live right. Live well, and you will be remembered well. Live the right kind of life, and you will leave the right kind of legacy.

Your Life's Purpose

Thinking About Your Talents, Opportunities, and Purpose
Everyone has a unique and special purpose in this world. Everyone is gifted with special qualities and abilities, each person is granted a unique set of talents and opportunities in life, and each individual has some valuable contribution that he can make to the lives of others. By identifying your unique talents, and also the things that you are passionate about and enjoy doing, you can begin to start understanding what your purpose in this world might be. This worksheet is designed to help you think about your purpose in life, by helping you think about the talents, abilities, and opportunities that you possess. It is meant to then help you figure out how to use each of those things, in order to make a difference in the world.

Determining Your Purpose In Life
So, how do you figure out what your purpose in life is?
Well, there are a couple of key questions that you should keep in mind throughout the next several years:

> 1. What things do I really have a passion for and enjoy doing?
> 2. What things am I really good at?
> 3. What does the world, or what do other people, need me to do?

~ When you find something that you have a passion for, that you are really
 good at, and that there is some need for in the world or in your community,
 then you will have found your purpose.

Think about and answer the following questions:

1. What do you have a passion for? What do you really enjoy doing?
     List 3 things that you really enjoy doing:
          1.
          2.
          3.

2. What are you really good at? What are some things that you do really well—better than others?
     List 3 things that you are really good at doing:
          1.
          2.
          3.

3. What might the world need you to do? What might other people need for you to do…
     How might other people need your help in order to succeed, or to make a better life for themselves?
          List 3 specific ways that you might be able to help other people:
          1.
          2.
          3.

The Two Most Important Days of Your Life
Someone famous once said, the two most important days of your life are…
   1. The day you were born, and
   2. The day you understand *why* you were born.

In other words: the day you were born *started* your life.
The day you figure out *why* you were born… is the day you can begin making the most of your life.

The Purpose of Living
The purpose of living is to do all that you can to reach your full potential in every regard, and to find a way to do it in service to some community that is larger than yourself. It is to do the absolute very best that you can do—at all times—to help enhance the world in which you live, and to positively impact the lives of those around you.

Start Thinking About Your Purpose In Life
Everyone has a specific purpose in this world. Once you start thinking about what that purpose might be, you are on your way to finding your role in the grand scheme of life. You don't have to figure it out right now. But it's always good to start thinking about it early on and to simply be aware of the concept.

Some Questions For You to Consider
What do you have a passion for? What types of things do you enjoy doing?
What are you good at? What are you able to excel and succeed at?
What special talents and abilities do you have?
What unique skills do you possess, that you enjoy putting to use and further developing?
What aspects of society do you wish to improve?
What does the world around you need in order to become a better and more positive place?

Another Important Consideration… What Has Shaped Your Ability to Shape the World?
What has impacted you in your lifetime? Is there something that has touched you personally, or someone who is close to you? Perhaps it is an illness, perhaps it is poverty, perhaps it is a positive mentor, or perhaps it is a unique opportunity; maybe it is a tragic event, maybe it is an incredibly inspiring role model, maybe it is a difficult period of adversity, or maybe it is a wonderful and life-changing experience.

Maybe you have a role model whose job you really admire… maybe you might want to think about trying that same career or profession. Maybe you have a friend or family member who is affected by cancer… maybe you might think about becoming a doctor to help cure cancer, or helping to raise money in order to help find a cure for cancer.

We each have unique experiences in our lives that draw our attention to something. Often, the events that shape our lives are what enable us to help shape the world around us. It's up to us to decide, first and foremost, if we are going to do anything about an issue, and secondly, HOW we are going to go about doing it…in other words, WHAT are we going to do to have some positive impact on the situation, and on the world around us? What can we do to positively affect our little corner of the world?

Live A Life That Matters… By Living for Something Greater Than Yourself
True significance in life depends on the service a person does for others, and not on what the individual achieves for himself. **It is service to others that fulfills one's true purpose in life.**

Make Your Life Count, and Make Your Life Matter
Make your life count for something, by accomplishing something worthwhile in your life.
Make your life matter to someone, by helping to improve the lives of those around you.

Who Cares How You Look? The Question Is... Can You PLAY?
It's not how you look, but how you play the game, that matters.

Focus On Your Contribution

If you look around the locker room prior to a game, you will see various members of the team getting suited up and ready for the competition that lies ahead.

Inevitably, there are always one or two student-athletes who can be found standing squarely in front of the mirror making sure they look good—making sure they "looked the part" of a play-maker. You know: they're the ones checking themselves out and flexing in front of the locker room mirror, checking to make sure their eye-black is applied just right, making sure their brand-name wristbands and armbands are pulled on just right, making sure their tape-jobs look good and straight, and making sure they look all big and puffed up... so they can impress everyone who comes to see them play... especially the ladies and all the fans in the stand. (Although, it bears asking: do you think the opposing strong safety or middle linebacker really cares how well-dressed you are, or how tight and legit you look... as he's getting ready to lay you out? Somehow, I don't think he cares.)

What some people unfortunately don't realize, is that what really matters is the production on the field, and not what anyone looks like when they are on the field. In other words: it is not about how you look, or how big you look; it is not about how much you talk, or about how big a game you can talk... ultimately, it is about what you can contribute. And it is about what you actually *do* contribute.

All the name-brand wristbands in the world don't mean a thing if you can't catch a football. All the eye-black in the sporting goods store won't matter an ounce if you can't block or tackle. All the apparel and accessories won't make a difference... if you, yourself, can't make a difference.

~

**Looking like a play-maker doesn't mean a thing.
It's *being* a play-maker that means everything. Anyone can talk a big game—anyone can talk about making a contribution. What really matters, though, is what you do when the lights come on. It's not who talks about making a contribution:
it's about who actually steps up and makes that contribution when it counts.**

~

A lot of times, we get so caught up in the surface things—the things that we think are important: things like our looks, our clothes, our image, our reputation, what other people think about us or say about us, and so on. However, none of those things are what really matter.

Now, do not get me wrong: sure it's nice to look good, it's nice to be able to dress well, it's nice to have people say good things about us, and it's nice to have a good reputation. But, just as is the case with competitive sports, what ultimately matters *the most* is the contribution we make.

Be a Play-Maker…
Play the Game of Life to the Best of Your Ability
It's not about how you look; it's about how you play the game.
And in the Game of Life, the same holds true. It's not about how you look—not about the clothes you wear, or the kicks (sneakers) you buy, or the watch you war, or even the car that you drive. It's about how you play the game—it's about how you live your life.
Anyone can *look* the part. But it takes a REAL man to PLAY the part.

It's not about how you look. It's about how well you can play your part.
It's about how well you can play the game. It's about how well you can live your life.

Talk is cheap… and Looks don't count for much.
It's how you play the game, that *really* speaks.

There are too many phonies out there already.
There are too many talkers to begin with.
What the world needs is do-ers.
What the world needs is people who are "play-makers,"
And not "prima-donnas."

Play-makers Wanted.

Be a "play-maker." Play the Game of Life to the best of your ability.
Live your life the best way that you can. Live it right, and live it well.
Live a life that matters… and Be a REAL man.

<u>**Achieve Success & Significance**</u>

Strive to achieve both success and significance in your life, by having a plan for your success, and by working to make yourself successful... By having a purpose for your life, and by working to fulfill your purpose in this life.

<u>Have a Plan.</u>
<u>Have a Purpose.</u>

Have a plan for your life.
Have ambition, direction, desire, and determination.
Set goals for yourself and for your life.
Set goals for who you want to become in your life.
Work hard to achieve your goals, and keep working until you make your dreams come true.

Have a plan for success, and work hard to become successful.
Decide what you want to achieve, and decide who you want to become.
Then determine to do all that you can to achieve your goals and accomplish your dreams.

Have a purpose for your life.
Live for something greater than yourself.
Develop yourself to the best of your ability, so that you can apply your talents and abilities in service to something that is bigger and greater than yourself. Invest in the lives of others, invest in the futures of others, invest in the successes of others... and you, yourself, will be a success as well. More importantly, you will be a significant influence on the people you meet, and on the world in which you live.

Have a purpose that goes beyond yourself. Figure out how you can make a difference.
Develop your talents and abilities, and use them to help others.

Be a man with a plan. Be a man on a mission.
Be a man with a purpose. Live with intention, and live with ambition.
Don't just go through the motions in life.
Live your life to the very absolute best of your ability.
Maximize your life, and help others to do the same.

Have a plan and have a purpose.

~ Have a plan and have a purpose.
　~ Have a plan for success, and work to become successful.
　　~ Have a purpose for your life, and work to become significant to the lives of others.
　　　~ Work to achieve success... but, more importantly, work to achieve significance.

Live with ambition, and live with purpose.
　Have a plan for yourself, and have a purpose for your life.
　　"Strong lives are motivated by dynamic purposes."
　　~ Kenneth Hildebrand

94

<u>Live A Life That Matters… By Making the Most of Your Life…</u>
Take responsibility for your life: Create your character and carve-out your destiny.

Take responsibility for your character… by taking responsibility for your attitude, by taking responsibility for your choices, by taking responsibility for your actions, and by taking responsibility for your habits.

Take responsibility for your destiny… By taking responsibility for your goals, by taking responsibility for your dreams… by taking responsibility for your commitment and hard work, and by taking responsibility for your effort and your determination.

Take responsibility of your life… by taking responsibility of everything that you think, do, and become in your life. Take responsibility for yourself, take responsibility for your life, and take control of your future.

<u>**Self-Actualization Worksheet**</u>

Self-Improvement for the Purpose of Self-Actualization:
Identifying Strengths & Weaknesses In Order to Work Toward Your Best Self
In order to reach your full potential and become everything that you are capable of becoming, you have to understand the strengths you already possess, and the weaknesses that you can (and should) improve upon. What follows, is a series of questions designed to help you identify your strengths and weaknesses, and to figure out how you can work to improve upon each. By understanding what you need to work on, and what ways you can improve upon yourself, you can begin to work toward reaching your full potential as a person… and ultimately, work to become everything that you are capable of becoming.

What are my three qualities that I am most proud of?

> List three of your greatest strengths:
>
> List three more of your good qualities:
>
> Why are these things important to me? Are they?
>
> How are these strengths and qualities helpful to helping me become successful?
>
> Is there anything you can do to *continue to develop* your strengths?
> What might you do?

What are three of my weaknesses, or flaws that I need to work on?

> List three weaknesses that you have:
>
> If you could, would you like to improve upon any of these weaknesses?
>
> How can you begin improving them? What can you do to work on your weaknesses?
>
> Why is it important to improve upon or change these things? Is it?
>
> Will improving upon your weaknesses help you to become successful? How?

My "Ideal Self" Worksheet

1. What are my biggest character strengths? (List at least 5)

      1.
      2.
      3.
      4.
      5.

2. What is my best character trait?

3. What words do I want to be described as or known for? What characteristics do I want to be known for? *(For example: Honest, Kind, Respectful, Responsible, a good Leader, someone who is Courageous, Someone who has Integrity, a Good Friend, Patient, Composed, Poised, etc.)* Try to pick at least 10.

4. What are my biggest weaknesses?

5. What characteristics do I *want* to be known for… **but right now I wouldn't honestly say that I possess?** (What characteristics do you want to develop that you don't have right now?)

6. Which <u>three character traits</u> do you think you need to **work on** *most*?
   (For example: Being responsible, being on-time, being honest, being respectful, being patient, being confident or believing in yourself, being positive, being polite to others, etc.)

      1.

      2.

      3.

Legacy Statement Worksheet

I want to be known for being _____
_____
_____
_____
_____

I want my biggest strength to be _____
_____

If other people had to describe me, and my life, in one sentence,
I would want them to be able to say:

_____
_____
_____
_____

(Example: One person's might be: "Here lies an honorable man.")

My Legacy Statement

Instructions: Write your own legacy statement below. Some questions to think about…
How do you want to be remembered? What do you want other people to be able to say
about who you are and about the way you lived your life?

_____
_____
_____
_____
_____
_____
_____
_____
_____
_____
_____
_____
_____
_____
_____
_____

The REAL Man Pledge

I Commit Myself to Being a REAL Man
I will do my very best, at all times, to be a REAL Man.

I will strive to:

* Respect all people,
* Especially women.
* Always do the right thing.
* Live a life that matters.

~

I will Answer the Call.
I will Stand Up and Stand Tall.
I will Be a REAL Man.
I will Make a REAL Difference.

Name _____

Signature _____   Date _____

The REAL Man Pledge

I Pledge to Always Be a REAL Man

I promise to:

* Respect all people,
* Especially women.
* Always do the right thing.
* Live a life that matters.

Name _____

Signature _____   Date _____

The REAL Man Team Pledge

We make a commitment as individuals, as a team, and as a family,
To live out the principles of what it means to truly be a REAL Man.

We make a commitment as individuals, as a team, and as a family,
To hold ourselves, our teammates, and our brothers accountable,
For living by, and living up to, the standards of a REAL Man.

Signatures:

_____   _____

_____   _____

_____   _____

_____   _____

_____   _____

_____   _____

_____   _____

_____   _____

_____   _____

_____   _____

_____   _____

_____   _____

The REAL Man Team Pledge

We make a commitment as individuals, as a team, and as a family,
To live out the principles of what it means to truly be a REAL Man.

We make a commitment as individuals, as a team, and as a family,
To hold ourselves, our teammates, and our brothers accountable,
For living by, and living up to, the standards of a REAL Man.

Signatures:

_____   _____

_____   _____

_____   _____

_____   _____

_____   _____

_____   _____

_____   _____

_____   _____

_____   _____

_____   _____

_____   _____

_____   _____

Exceed Expectations: Be More than What the World Wants, Be What It Needs

Society doesn't expect much from its men. But the world *needs* great men, *real* men.
The people of this world need boys who will grow up and *stand up*, and be *real* men.
Forget about what the world *expects* you to be; focus on being who the world *needs* you to be.

So, in order to do this, you must cast aside all those false ideas out there about what being a man is all about. You have to recognize—all of us have to recognize—that the myths that are out there are flat wrong: that being a man has nothing to do with the money you make, or the women you get, or the things you can buy, or the cars you can drive. Being a real man has nothing to do with those things, and it has everything to do with the way you live your life.

And that's exactly what it is: *your* life.
It's not society's. It's not other people's. It's yours.
So don't settle for other people's expectations of you.
Don't settle for what society thinks is enough from you.
Be yourself. Have the courage to stand up and to live your life the right way.

Wise Words from the World's Great Leaders

Dr. Martin Luther King, Jr. once said: "We are called to be non-conformists"

In his letter to the Romans, the apostle Paul "Do not conform to the pattern of this world, but be transformed by the renewing of your mind." To put it another way…

"Don't copy the behaviors and customs of this world, but be a new and different person with a fresh newness in all you do and think." – Romans 12:2 TLB
    In other words: Be an original. Be yourself. Be REAL, and be the REAL you.

To echo Paul's sentiments: "Don't let the world around you squeeze you into its own mold."
~ Romans 12:2 PHI

Be REAL, and Be the REAL You

You have to be yourself. You have to dictate your own character.
Don't let the world do it for you. You dictate your own attitude—the right attitude.
You dictate your own decisions—the *right* decisions.
You dictate your own actions—the *right* actions.
You dictate the way you treat other people—the *right* way.
You dictate the way you live your life—the right way, and the absolute best way you know how.
Don't settle for other people's expectations. Go above and beyond what society expects.

Exceed Expectations. Don't be satisfied with what the world thinks is acceptable. **Stand up!**
Do more than what society expects you to do. *Be more* than what society expects you to be. Don't just settle for the bare minimum: be something special.
Be someone special. Do something special with your life.

Do You Have What It Takes To Be A Real Man?

The world needs Real Men … Men who will stand up and make a difference.
 Will you answer the challenge? Will you stand up and be a <u>Real</u> man?
    "The question is not can you change the world around you.
    The only question is ***will you decide to do so***." ~ Jeffrey Marx

ARE YOU FOR *REAL* ?

If You Want To Be A
~ REAL Man ~

There are a lot of myths in our society about what it means to be a real man. Contrary to popular belief, being a man is not about how strong and muscular you are; it's not about what kind of car you drive; it's not about how much money you have, or about how many women you can use.

Life is not about money, cars, fame, physical appearance, and women. It's about who you are as a person; it's about the way you live your life; and it's about how you treat other people.

When it comes right down to it…

Being a **REAL** man means that you:

R-espect all people,

E-specially women.

A-lways do the right thing.

L-ive a life that matters.

BE A REAL MAN

MAKE A REAL DIFFERENCE

~

RESPECT ALL PEOPLE

Show respect to all people, at all times, in all ways.
Treat others the way you would want to be treated.
Respect yourself and always carry yourself with class.

ESPECIALLY WOMEN

Treat women with the utmost respect.
Be a gentleman at all times. Be respectful in all ways.
Accept women. Respect women. Protect women.

ALWAYS DO THE RIGHT THING

Have the courage to do the right thing.
Always be yourself. Always keep your word.
Live by your principles. Honor your commitments.

LIVE A LIFE THAT MATTERS

Live with honor. Live with purpose. Live with determination.
Be a role model. Make a difference in the lives of others.
Leave a legacy. Live for something greater than yourself.

~

Stand Up and Stand Tall:
~ **Be a REAL Man!** ~

If You Want To Be A
~ REAL Woman ~

There are a lot of myths in our society about what it means to be a real woman. Contrary to popular belief, being a woman is not about how pretty or skinny you are; it's not about what kind of clothes you wear; it's not about how much money you have, or about how much you can by with that money.

Life is not about popularity, fame, money, or clothes. It's not about looks, accessories, or physical appearance. It's about who you are as a person; it's about how you live your life, and it's about how you treat other people.

When it comes right down to it…

Being a **REAL** woman means that you:

R-espect all people,
E-specially yourself.
A-lways do the right thing.
L-ive a life that matters.

BE A **REAL** WOMAN

MAKE A REAL DIFFERENCE

~

RESPECT ALL PEOPLE

Show respect to all people, at all times, in all ways.
Treat others the way you would want to be treated.
Speak well of others. Refrain from gossiping about others.

ESPECIALLY YOURSELF

Accept yourself. Respect yourself. Love yourself.
Value yourself. Cherish yourself. Honor yourself.
Always be a lady. Always be classy and respectable.

ALWAYS DO THE RIGHT THING

Have the courage to do the right thing.
Always be yourself. Always keep your word.
Live by your principles. Honor your commitments.

LIVE A LIFE THAT MATTERS

Live with honor. Live with purpose. Live with determination.
Be a role model. Make a difference in the lives of others.
Leave a legacy. Live for something greater than yourself.

~

Always be classy. Always be respectable.
~ Always Be a REAL Woman! ~

Made in the USA
Charleston, SC
07 January 2013